Faster! I'm Starving!

Faster! I'm Starving!

100 Dishes in 25 Minutes or Less

Kevin Mills and Nancy Mills

Authors of
Help! My Apartment Has a Kitchen!

Gibbs Smith, Publisher
Salt Lake City

First Edition

10 09 08 07 06   5 4 3 2

Text © 2006 Kevin Mills and Nancy Mills

Published by
Gibbs Smith, Publisher
P.O. Box 667
Layton, Utah 84041

Orders: 1.800.748.5439
www.gibbs-smith.com

Designed by Don Manley
Printed and bound in the U.S.A.

Library of Congress Cataloging-in-Publication Data
Mills, Kevin, 1971-
Faster! I'm starving! : 100 dishes in 25 minutes or less / Kevin Mills and Nancy Mills.— 1st ed.
    p. cm.
Includes index.
ISBN 1-58685-795-9
1. Quick and easy cookery. I. Mills, Nancy, 1942- II. Title.

TX833.5.M553 2006
641.5'55—dc22

                    2005025800

We would like to dedicate this book to Bonnie and Tom Trenga, our tasters and testers.

Thanks also go to Jody Kraft and Bart Mills for their patient palates, and to Melissa Barlow, Madge Baird and Jennifer Grillone for believing in us. And finally, for recipe contributions we would like to acknowledge Jim Bergschneider, Fernanda Capraro, Allison Rodd Ceppi, Kelly DiNardo, Steve Dunhoff, Ekta Farrar, Cindy Froggatt, Ruki Ghaznavi, Lynne Giviskos, Sue Hagen, Joy Higa, Julie Lipsius, Kathy McCullough, Carol Mead, Martha Mills, Mary Morigaki, Judy Rich, Steve Riskin, Dorothy Samuel and Jane Townsend.

Also a special thanks to Joey, Andy and Sammy, who love to help. Although to them cooking is an art project (the messier, the better), it's always fun to have them in the kitchen.

Contents

Panic Time in the Kitchen

I know how to cook, but I'm even better at ordering out. I can bake, I can fry, I can sauté, but I'm unbelievable at ripping off the tops of boxes and sticking frozen dinners in the microwave. And I could teach a class on how to sit in line at a drive-thru.

I prefer a home-cooked meal, but there are so many easy ways out in today's world. It's a dilemma that my wife and I deal with seemingly every evening. We live within ten minutes of about 700 restaurants, fast-food chains and frozen food aisles. They beckon, they tempt, they mock, and we try to resist.

Does our predicament sound familiar? Do you wish you had the time, talent and inclination to create magnificent feasts that would make Emeril break down and weep in envy, but instead often settle for boiling water and pouring it into a styrofoam cup filled with dried noodles and flavor crystals? Thankfully, my mom showed me that there is a middle road.

Mom never seems to have this dilemma at dinnertime. She cooks every night, and has since I was in a high chair. I grew up watching her create three-course meals effortlessly, keeping three or four pots going at different heats, cracking eggs with the left hand while stirring with the right. I didn't always appreciate the variety and quality of what she cooked—I wanted to have spaghetti every night.

My mom seems to live in fear, and has since I was born, that I'm not eating properly. And as much as I hate to admit it, without her help she'd probably be right. Over the last decade she's made a cook out of me, even if I was reluctant at every step. But now I'm so busy that I hardly have time to cook. Upon hearing this news, mom climbed on her magic whisk and flew through my window to continue a process she began almost a decade ago.

It all started when I finished college and moved in with my girlfriend. For the first few years it was like we were playing house. We put together a kitchen from hand-me-down pots and pans and stolen dining-hall silverware. When we'd cook, it was more like we were lab partners in a chemistry class than real chefs. We still mostly ate out and ordered in, so when we cooked it was a very special occasion. Sometimes the food even tasted good.

That was when we were in our early twenties. My mom took it upon herself to send us recipes that would be difficult to ruin. By then I'd (mostly) gotten over my adolescent rejection of all motherly advice, and I accepted her help in learning how to cook a few starvation-preventers like roast chicken and lasagna. At that point mom and I decided to write our first cookbook, which became *Help! My Apartment Has a Kitchen*. It documented that early period when she first convinced me that I couldn't keep eating like I was at summer camp.

Then my girlfriend became my wife, we passed twenty-five and now were both adults even in our own minds. At this point in life, eating is no longer just something you do while watching *The Simpsons* in bed. Adults, for some reason, like to eat in groups. And so we had to start cooking for other married couples, which required a new level of variety and polish in our cooking. I'd already written a cookbook, but I still felt like a novice in the kitchen. So my mom continued her teaching process, and *Help! My Apartment Has a Dining Room* was born. Once again my cooking progress was tied to both my expanding taste in food and the expectations placed on me by my increasing years.

Our next collaboration involved a side trip into self-indulgence. Both mom and I are lunatic chocolate eaters, and we fully explored this passion in *Chocolate on the Brain*. My progress in the kitchen had reached the point that I was able to follow more complicated recipes, but I would only do so if, when I was done, I could swim the backstroke in pools of chocolate excess.

But then, in my late twenties, a few things happened. First, I needed to get an exercise bike to work off the effects of eating too many chocolate desserts for breakfast. And second, my wife and I had a baby. It began the most recent phase of our lives wherein time was a much more precious resource. Of course I love everything about fatherhood—especially tantrums and middle-of-the-night diaper changes—but I do miss having a few minutes of peace and quiet. And Joey's birth, followed a few years later by Andy's and then Sammy's, has inspired the need for the latest evolution in my cooking experience.

My wife and I found ourselves eating spaghetti five nights a week. What I'd thought would be the perfect diet as a child actually turned out to be extremely boring. And some nights, especially when my wife worked late, even spaghetti was too much work. Our options were reduced to calling for pizza at 10 p.m. or just sitting on the kitchen floor and stuffing fistfuls of American cheese in our mouths. We needed more quick, easy foods. Once again, mom was ready with recipes and advice.

Faster! I'm Starving! comes from this place in our lives, where my wife and I need to cook in as little time as possible. Our youthful laziness has given way to grown-up busyness, and if we can cook a complete meal in 25 minutes or less, we will resist the temptation to take the easy way out.

My mom's solutions involve recipes with limited preparation required, techniques to fast-forward through chopping and cleaning, and ways to intensify and quicken the cooking process. And we're not talking about hotdogs and cheeseburgers here. Instead, we have Pasta and Bean Soup, Chinese-Style Pork Medallions and Roasted Portobello Mushroom Burgers. These are one-dish meals that we couldn't get at a fast-food chain if we wanted to.

So now, with the latest recipes and techniques my mom has given us, we can cook a healthy, interesting dinner within the length of a sitcom. These dinners taste good enough to keep us from surrendering to the temptations just down the street. And they're easy enough to make with a baby in one arm and two little boys holding onto each leg, which is a must for us.

I've been cooking for ten years now, but I'm still learning. Maybe by the time I'm in a nursing home I'll be completely comfortable in the kitchen. Hopefully by then my mom and I will have written a book about how to cook food that you can eat without teeth. But until then, my tastes and abilities, like yours probably, will continue to evolve. I hope this book helps you eat well while you go about living your lives.

—Kevin Mills

Techniques Geared for Speed

Preparation

In the interest of speed, I suggested we could cut vegetables with a chainsaw and then cook them with a blowtorch. But maybe it's best that mom does the thinking for the two of us. Her techniques are more subtle and effective. Occasionally her suggestions are a bit more expensive, but they can save a lot of time and effort.

Buy Ingredients Partly Prepared

Prewashed bags of lettuce: Sometimes I worry when I buy packaged foods that they've had their taste removed and replaced with four-syllable preservatives. That's not the case here. The lettuce growers have done all the work.

Bags of trimmed, fresh baby carrots: There they are, already peeled, washed and bite-size. Plus, they have a cute name.

Precut fresh broccoli, cauliflower and other salad bar ingredients: Much easier, more hygienic and certainly more legal than taking zipper-lock bags and absconding with veggies from the salad bar at Wendy's.

Frozen chopped onions: Save yourself the tears of cutting onions.

Precooked bacon: A real time-saver, although I miss the smell of bacon cooking.

Grated cheeses: These cheeses can spoil faster, but when you're in a hurry, who wants to grate a block of cheese? To keep the mold away, store grated cheese in the freezer.

Bottles of crushed fresh garlic: Some cooks swear by fresh garlic, but when you're in a hurry, bottled crushed garlic is very useful. As fun as it is to squeeze garlic through a press, I haven't bothered to prepare my own garlic for years.

Bottles of crushed fresh ginger: These are especially useful if you don't use ginger very often, which I don't.

Surimi: I'd never heard of this, but mom turned me on to it. It's also called imitation crab or krab. It's a precooked white fish sold loose at some fish counters but more commonly found in vacuum-sealed packages. It's an inexpensive substitute for lobster and crab, and there are no bones or claws.

Sausages: Sausages are often available precooked. They're useful as a stand-alone meal or as a protein addition to soups or salads.

Cold cuts: Cold cuts such as sliced turkey, roast beef or ham have lots of last-minute uses, including fillings for omelets or tortillas. They can also stretch a side salad into a main dish salad.

Smaller and Thinner Means Faster Cooking

The more surface that is exposed to heat, the faster it cooks. That's just common sense. Just ask anyone who's lain out in the sun too long. The same principle applies to food. Here are some tips on speeding things up by making ingredients smaller and thinner:

※ It's easier to cut chicken and beef into thin slices or strips when the meat is partly frozen. Plus, you don't have to wait for the meat to completely thaw before cooking it.

※ If you cut boneless chicken breasts in half crosswise through the middle to make two thinner chicken breasts, they will cook nearly twice as fast. If you cut them into three slices, they will cook even faster or within minutes.

※ Steak or chicken cut into 2-inch-long, 1/2 inch-wide strips can be stir-fried in 2–3 minutes.

※ Ground meat cooks much faster than whole pieces of meat.

※ Thin slices of vegetables cook faster. For instance, very thin potato slices cook in less than 10 minutes in soups, whereas a whole potato will take 20–25 minutes.

✳ Grated potatoes or other vegetables will cook faster still, a little-known fact useful when making Parmesan Potato Pancakes (page 222). To save even more time, buy packaged, fresh-grated potatoes.

✳ Pound meat thinner. Boneless chicken and pork will cook more quickly the thinner it is. Just check the cooking times on such recipes as Chinese-Style Pork Medallions (page 168) and Chinese Lemon Chicken (page 138). Pound the meat between sheets of wax paper with a rolling pin or the side of a heavy can. Merely sitting on it won't work.

Techniques for Cutting Very Quickly

Mom can operate a knife like the android in *Aliens*. But when I try to speed up my chopping, my fingertips are in mortal danger. With mom's advice, you can keep the antiseptic in the medicine cabinet.

You can chop vegetables in the food processor by using the pulse button—although you have to be careful they don't turn to mush. Or use the slicing disc attachment. You might not want to bother if you're just cutting up a handful of vegetables, but for bulk slicing it's a real time-saver. I recommend you use it for onions and save yourself a couple of hankies.

You can also turn your blender into a chopping device. Half-fill the blender with water. Roughly cut the vegetables into 2-inch pieces, add them to the blender and pulse until they are the size you want. Then drain the contents of the blender into a strainer.

To cut celery quickly, wash the whole head (all the stalks together, still attached), trim and discard the top 1/2 inch of stalks. Then thinly slice through all the stalks at once until you have the amount of celery you need. Don't worry about all the pieces being identical.

Cooking

When you want to get food on the table in 25 minutes or less, there are certain kinds of dishes you won't be eating. No beef stews. No roast turkeys. No barbecued pork. Some cooking techniques just can't be speeded up. In certain cases, however, you can change an ingredient or a cooking technique, which will speed up the cooking process. For instance, we've adapted the traditionally long-cooking French beef stew called Beef Bourguignon into a 20-minute version (page 164) using sirloin steak instead of stewing beef.

Stir-frying

Stir-frying, which is basically frying small pieces of meat and/or vegetables on a large, hot surface, need not be limited to a wok. A large frying pan or griddle can work equally as well. Don't stop stirring while you're frying, though, or you might need a chisel and a hammer to remove the food from the surface.

High-Temperature Roasting

Cookbook author Barbara Kafka perfected a technique of roasting meat at 500 degrees F to shorten cooking times. It makes a mess of the oven and she says she cleans hers every night. But this high-temperature technique does allow us to meet our deadline on Roast Beef in 20 Minutes (page 182). Besides, I don't really care how clean my oven is. If it was spotless, it would seem out of place in my house. An oven needs a few battle scars.

Gas Grill Grilling

Because a gas grill takes only a few minutes to heat up, you can cook Grilled Steak Slices (page 178) or Greek Lambburgers (page 154) in minutes. It can be a real boon to the cook in a hurry.

Speedy Ingredients

We're all looking for shortcuts—get-rich-quick schemes, get-thin-quick diets, machines that flatten your abs while you read the newspaper. Well, I can't vouch for any of those shortcuts. But there are shortcuts you can take in cooking to speed up the process. Substitute some of these ingredients in your favorite recipes in order to speed up the cooking.

Boneless chicken breasts: A boneless chicken breast is the most versatile item at the meat counter. Although it tastes best fresh, it can be kept frozen for six months. It can be sliced and diced in a half-frozen state. It can be boiled from a frozen state and be ready to eat in 25 minutes. It can be roasted, stir-fried, pan-fried and grilled. It can be eaten plain or with a variety of sauces.

Boneless chicken breasts are often on sale and are always low in calories. My mom reads the grocery ads so closely that I suspect she holds them up to the light to see hidden values. Whenever she spots boneless chicken breasts on sale, she camps out outside the store and comes home with a freezer-full.

Sirloin steak: Most people think of steak simply as a grilled or broiled cut of meat, but it's much more versatile than that. Because this cut is tender and cooks quickly, it can be cut up and used in stir-fries. It can also be substituted for long-cooking cuts of beef to make Short-Cut Beef Bourguignon (page 164). In addition to sirloin steak, you can use any steak that you would broil or grill, including New York strip, shell, T-bone, porterhouse, rib, rib eye or Delmonico.

Pork tenderloin: Pork tenderloin is another versatile cut of meat. A lot of cooks may not know this cut, which looks like a miniature baseball bat and is usually packaged in vacuum-sealed plastic. It's the most expensive cut of pork, but since it's boneless there is virtually no waste. It can be roasted, grilled or sliced and fried even faster than boneless chicken breasts.

Ground beef, lamb, pork, chicken and turkey: Ground meat cooks very quickly and can be a mainstay for the harried cook. Burgers can be more than just ketchup-slathered beef disks with a pickle slice on top. There are many different varieties like Popeye Turkeyburgers (page 126) or Greek Lambburgers (page 154). You can also use a small amount of ground meat to bulk up a meal—add it to a pasta sauce or a soup, or crumble a leftover burger to make a quick Taco Salad (page 46).

Shrimp (fresh or frozen): Shrimp can be a dinner lifesaver. Frozen cooked shrimp can be dropped into a pot of boiling water for 1 minute to thaw. Frozen uncooked shrimp need just 3–5 minutes to cook. I prefer to buy them already cleaned and frozen. This way you won't have to remove the little legs (eww). Shrimp can be eaten with cocktail sauce, added to a vegetable stir-fry or pasta, or can be the basis of a dish like Coconut Shrimp Curry (page 202).

Scallops (fresh or frozen): Scallops are expensive, although thumbnail-size scallops are sometimes sold for as little as 5 dollars a pound. A bag of frozen scallops is useful in an emergency. Scallops go from frozen to cooked in under 5 minutes and fit right into a dish like Basil and Scallop Linguine (page 86).

Fish: Fish cooks very quickly. You can bake it, fry it, grill it and use it in soups, and it's usually ready in less than 10 minutes. As a diner, I've always been uptight about fish because I hate to have to remove a piece of skeleton while I'm eating dinner. But mom has some useful tips that make this fast-cooking food easy to deal with.

Eggs: Everybody keeps eggs around, except for lacto-vegetarians and vegans, and I honestly don't know what they eat. The eggs that are sitting in your fridge can be very versatile. Omelets (page 78) and Mushroom and Zucchini Frittatas (page 76) can make full meals, and, in a true emergency, fried eggs on toast will fill me up. Eggs are essential for Pasta Carbonara (page 94) and Indian Fried Rice (page 106).

Couscous: This North African staple is made out of the same ingredients as pasta. Traditional couscous can take 45 minutes to prepare, but the almost-instant version, available in boxes either near the rice or in the ethnic foods aisle, cooks in 5 minutes. It's a handy substitute for rice or potatoes.

Fresh pasta: If you make your own pasta, you won't eat until tomorrow. But ready-made fresh pasta takes about half as long to cook as dried pasta. Angel hair is the fastest-cooking fresh pasta, at 1 minute. Fresh pasta freezes well, and you can cook it almost as quickly from its frozen state. Because fresh pasta is heavier than dried pasta, you need to plan for about 6 ounces per person instead of 2 to 3 ounces per person for dried pasta.

Cellophane noodles and dried rice sticks: These Asian staples cook almost instantly. Read the directions on the labels. In some cases, you can "cook" them by simply soaking them in water for a few minutes.

Instant potatoes: Fans of lumpy mashed potatoes will never get used to the instant variety, but they are incredibly convenient when you're in a hurry. In addition to simple mashed potatoes, instant potatoes are useful for thickening soups. There also isn't the sacrifice in taste that you get with instant rice.

Orzo: A quick-cooking dried pasta (it takes just 9 minutes) that looks like rice, orzo goes with just about everything.

Canned Foods That Are Incredibly Time-Saving:

Broth: Chicken, beef and vegetable broth are pantry staples. Maybe they're not as good as the homemade kind my grandmother makes, but if you have time to make homemade broth you're probably not reading this book. Bouillon cubes and bouillon granules are also useful. Dissolve 2 cubes or 2 teaspoons in 2 cups water as a substitute for a 14-ounce can of broth. Chicken, beef and vegetable base—a concentrated bouillon paste—is available in 8- and 16-ounce jars at some grocery stores and specialty food shops. It is very convenient when you need a small amount of broth. Just spoon out what you need and mix it with water, as directed on the jar.

Tomatoes: My mom talks about not being able to live without ready-cut canned tomatoes. I'd probably find a reason to carry on, but they are awfully convenient and are useful in so many recipes.

Boneless salmon (a good emergency food): Use it to make Deviled Salmon Patties (page 190).

Smoked fish (kipper or trout fillets): I was born in England, and while our family lived there we developed a taste for smoked fish, which was readily available at the fishmonger's. Canned smoked fish is stocked in American grocery stores near the tuna. Mom uses this fish to make Indian Fried Rice (page 106), a dish the British call Kedgeree.

Clams: Linguine with White Clam Sauce (page 92) is the one meal my dad can cook, so whenever my mom would go out of town, my sister and I knew what was coming. I was surprised to find out later in life that clams could be used in other dishes, like Creamy Fish Chowder (page 26).

Canned beans: Canned beans save hours of cooking time. They can be the basis of a meal such as Red Beans and Rice (page 110) or Calamari Salad (page 38), or they can be filling additions to main-dish soups like Garbanzo Bean and Tomato Soup (page 28) and Pasta and Bean Soup (page 32).

Prepared sauces: In addition to a pasta topping, spaghetti sauce can easily substitute in recipes that call for homemade tomato sauce. My mom and my wife both love an Indian masala simmer sauce that they discovered at Trader Joe's, a gourmet food market. Is it still cooking if you're using a prepared sauce? I say yes, unless you're drinking the sauce straight from the jar. And if you are, I don't think even my mom can help you.

Helpful Equipment

Why make things difficult? Here are some gadgets that are easily available that do the work for you.

Blender: A blender is particularly useful for soups, although you can also use it to chop vegetables.

Food processor: A food processor is useful for many things, including slicing, chopping and shredding vegetables and cheese and grinding up mixtures.

Mini food processor: A mini food processor is convenient for small chopping jobs, and it requires much less cleaning than its big brother.

Handheld blender (immersion blender): A handheld blender is a useful tool for making soup. Besides, it's just cool. My wife tries to come up with reasons to use it.

Microwave: A microwave is invaluable for defrosting meat and reheating leftovers. How else can you have a baked potato ready in less than 10 minutes? However, this book relies on the microwave only minimally for cooking.

Soups

There are many kinds of soups—thick ones, thin ones, chunky ones and creamy ones. The only thing that unites them is that you eat them with a spoon. We have them all in this section. From the vegetarian Pasta and Bean Soup to the very meaty Polish Sausage Soup, you can be sure of one thing: These aren't dainty appetizers. These soups will fill you up.

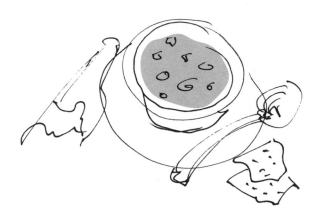

Beefy Meatball and Egg Noodle Soup

Cantonese Fish Soup

Creamy Fish Chowder

Garbanzo Bean and Tomato Soup

Hefty Lentil Soup

Pasta and Bean Soup

Polish Sausage Soup

Beefy Meatball and Egg Noodle Soup

Serves: 3–4 *

Preparation time: 10 minutes *

Cooking time: 14 minutes *

Time-saving tip: Use packaged, prewashed spinach. *

No soup can be everything to all people. But this soup will be something to most people. It's very filling, has meatballs, noodles, mushrooms and spinach, and it cooks much faster than you'd expect for such a substantial meal. Put those cup-o-soups back in the cupboard forever.

1 14-ounce can beef broth plus 1 can water OR 2 beef bouillon cubes, 2 teaspoons beef bouillon granules or 2 teaspoons beef base plus 3 cups water

1 tablespoon soy sauce

1 teaspoon bottled ginger or 1/2 teaspoon ground ginger

2 scallions

1/2 pound ground sirloin or very lean beef

1 teaspoon cornstarch

1/4 teaspoon black pepper

3 ounces uncooked medium egg noodles (about 1 1/2 cups)

1/2 pound presliced mushrooms

2 cups fresh spinach

Put the beef broth, water, soy sauce and ginger into a medium pot and begin heating over medium-high heat.

Meanwhile, rinse and trim the scallions and cut them into 1/4-inch pieces. Put the scallions, beef, cornstarch and black pepper into a small bowl and mix well with a fork or your fingers. Shape the mixture into 30 to 35 marble-sized meatballs, about 1 inch in diameter. Or, to save time, make larger meatballs.

Bring the broth to a boil and then add the meatballs and noodles. Don't worry if some of the scallion pieces fall out of the meatballs. When it returns to a boil, turn down to medium-high heat and cook, uncovered, for 5 minutes, stirring occasionally. Add the mushrooms and cook 5 minutes more. Add the spinach and cook another 2 minutes, or until it wilts, stirring occasionally. Serve immediately. Or set aside until ready to eat, and then reheat briefly.

Cantonese Fish Soup

Serves: 3–4 ✳

Preparation time: 10 minutes ✳

Cooking time: 13 minutes ✳

Time-saving tip: Use 3/4 cup leftover rice and 2 cups frozen cauliflower or precut cauliflower from the grocery store's salad bar. ✳

I've probably had Chinese takeout more times in my life than I've exercised. But eating all that Chinese food hasn't translated into being able to cook it. Cantonese Fish Soup isn't complicated. In addition to its ease of preparation and good taste, this recipe has two advantages: it isn't as spicy as a lot of Chinese soups and it doesn't come in a leaky cardboard container.

2 14-ounce cans chicken broth OR 3 chicken bouillon cubes, 3 teaspoons chicken bouillon granules or 3 teaspoons chicken base plus 3 1/2 cups water

1/4 cup uncooked white rice

1/2 small cauliflower

1 pound white fish fillets (see Mom Tip)

1/4 cup frozen green peas

1 tablespoon soy sauce

1 teaspoon bottled ginger or 1/2 teaspoon ground ginger

3 scallions

1 large egg

Put the chicken broth and rice into a large pot and begin heating over high heat. When the broth comes to a boil, turn down to medium heat, cover and cook for 5 minutes.

Trim and discard the leaves and core from the cauliflower. Cut the rest into bite-size pieces and then set aside.

Cut the fish into 2-inch chunks. Remove and discard any visible bones.

Add the cauliflower, fish, peas, soy sauce and ginger to the rice mixture and bring to a boil over high heat. Turn down to medium heat and cook, covered, about 5 minutes, or until the fish can be separated into flakes.

While the soup is cooking, rinse and trim the scallions and cut them into 1/4-inch pieces. Beat the egg in a small dish.

When the fish is cooked, pour the egg slowly into the hot broth and stir about 20 seconds, or until the egg cooks and forms thin strands. Add the scallions and serve immediately. Or set aside until ready to eat, and then reheat briefly.

Mom Tip: Tilapia, catfish or sole fillets, which are thin, will cook in 5 minutes. Cod, red snapper or sea bass, which are thicker, will take a few minutes longer.

Creamy Fish Chowder

Serves: 4 ✳

Preparation time: 15 minutes ✳

Cooking time: 10 minutes ✳

Time-saving tip: Use packaged fresh grated potatoes and frozen chopped onions. Don't catch your own fish. ✳

This soup isn't a dainty appetizer. It's a loosen-your-belt, take-a-nap-afterward kind of soup. Put on your yellow rain slicker, turn on a CD of your favorite sea shanties and dig in.

1 large onion

2 large potatoes

1 tablespoon olive or corn oil

1 teaspoon bottled crushed garlic

1 teaspoon cornstarch

8 slices precooked bacon

1 1/2 pounds fish fillets (any white fish or salmon, or a mixture of fish)

1 14-ounce can chicken broth OR 2 chicken bouillon cubes, 2 teaspoons chicken bouillon granules or 2 teaspoons chicken base plus 2 cups water

1/2 teaspoon ground thyme

1/2 teaspoon salt

1/4 teaspoon black pepper

1/2 pound cooked shrimp

1 6 1/2-ounce can chopped or minced clams

1/2 cup heavy cream (see Mom Tip 1)

Handful fresh spinach (optional)

Peel the onion and potatoes and cut them into 1/2-inch pieces. Put the oil into a large pot and begin heating over medium-high heat. Add the onion, potatoes and garlic and cook about 5 minutes, stirring occasionally, or until the vegetables begin to soften. Add the cornstarch and stir until it dissolves.

Cut the bacon and the fish into 1-inch pieces with kitchen scissors. Add the chicken broth, bacon, fish, thyme, salt and black pepper and cook for 5 minutes. Add the shrimp, clams and their juice, cream and spinach, if using, and stir to incorporate. Continue heating the soup until hot and serve immediately. Or set aside until ready to eat, and then reheat briefly.

Mom Tip 1: Evaporated milk can substitute for heavy cream in a soup.

Mom Tip 2: The soup should be thick and chunky. If it seems too watery, stir in 1 or 2 tablespoons instant potato flakes and cook another minute so it thickens slightly.

Garbanzo Bean and Tomato Soup

Serves: 4 ✳

Preparation time: 10 minutes ✳

Cooking time: 15 minutes ✳

Time-saving tip: Use frozen chopped onions. ✳

One-dish meals are highly prized in our house. If my wife and I find a recipe that we both like, fills us both up, AND only requires us to clean one pot and a cutting board, we know we have a keeper. Garbanzo Bean and Tomato Soup meets all the above criteria to make a perfect one-dish meal.

1 large onion

2 tablespoons olive or corn oil

1 tablespoon bottled crushed garlic

1/2 teaspoon black pepper

1/4 teaspoon red pepper flakes

1 15-ounce can ready-cut tomatoes

3 14-ounce cans vegetable broth OR 5 vegetable bouillon cubes, 5 teaspoons vegetable bouillon granules or 5 teaspoons vegetable base plus 5 1/4 cups water

1 tablespoon bottled lemon juice

2 15-ounce cans garbanzo beans

1 6-ounce bag (about 8 cups) fresh prewashed spinach

Grated Parmesan cheese

Peel the onion and cut it into 1/2-inch pieces. Put the oil into a large pot and begin heating over medium-high heat. Add the onion and cook about 5 minutes, stirring occasionally, or until it begins to soften.

Add the garlic, black pepper and red pepper flakes and stir briefly. Add the tomatoes and their juice and continue cooking for 5 minutes. Then add the vegetable broth and lemon juice and bring the mixture to a boil over high heat. While the mixture is heating, drain the garbanzo beans, rinse them under cold running water and then add them to the pot.

When the mixture returns to a boil, add the spinach and stir for a few seconds until it wilts. If the soup seems too thick for your taste, add 1/2 to 1 cup water and heat until hot. Serve immediately with Parmesan cheese sprinkled over top. Or set aside until ready to eat, and then reheat briefly.

Mom Tip: Add 1/2 to 1 cup leftover cooked pasta or rice to make the soup even more filling.

Hefty Lentil Soup

Serves: 4 ✳

Preparation time: 10 minutes (overlaps with cooking time) ✳

Cooking time: 20 minutes ✳

Time-saving tip: Use frozen chopped onions. ✳

Why is this soup called Hefty Lentil Soup, and not Hefty Potato Soup or Hefty Onion Soup? Did we just pick one, or did the lentil people get to us? We'll never tell. P.S. Eat lentils. Can't get enough of that lentil goodness. Oh, I guess onions and potatoes are pretty good, too. Anyway, this soup is a great meal-in-one that passes the spoon-standing-up test.

2 14-ounce cans chicken, beef or vegetable broth OR 3 chicken, beef or vegetable bouillon cubes, 3 teaspoons chicken, beef or vegetable bouillon granules or 3 teaspoons chicken, beef or vegetable base plus 3 1/2 cups water

1 cup dried lentils

1 large onion

1 medium potato

1 tablespoon olive oil

1 teaspoon bottled crushed garlic

1 teaspoon ground coriander

1 teaspoon ground cumin

1 teaspoon salt

1 teaspoon bottled ginger or 1/2 teaspoon ground ginger

1/4 teaspoon red pepper flakes

1/4 teaspoon black pepper

Put the broth and lentils into a large pot and bring to a boil over high heat. Turn down to low heat and cook, covered, about 20 minutes, or until the lentils are soft enough to chew.

While the mixture is cooking, peel the onion and potato and cut them into 1/4-inch pieces. Put the olive oil into a small frying pan and begin heating over medium-high heat. Add the onion, potato and garlic and cook about 5 minutes, stirring occasionally, or until vegetables begin to soften.

Add the coriander, cumin, salt, ginger, red pepper flakes and black pepper to the frying pan and stir briefly. Set aside until the lentils have finished cooking. Add the onion mixture to the lentils and stir thoroughly.

If the soup seems too thick for your taste, add 1/2 to 1 cup water and heat until hot. Serve immediately. Or set aside until ready to eat, and then reheat briefly.

Mom Tip: To make this soup even more hefty, add 1 cup frozen cooked shrimp about 3 minutes before serving. Continue cooking until they thaw.

Pasta and Bean Soup

Serves: 3–4 ✳

Preparation time: 14 minutes ✳

Cooking time: 10–11 minutes ✳

Time-saving tip: Use leftover pasta or substitute 1 cup leftover rice for pasta. ✳

At the risk of going to war with Italy, we've changed the name of this soup from the original Pasta e Fagioli. As Pasta and Bean Soup, it's clear that it's a simple, filling, one-dish meal. It even includes vegetables. You can change the name back if you're serving it to company.

2 large carrots

1 large onion

2 ounces prosciutto

1 tablespoon olive or corn oil

1 15-ounce can cannellini, pinto or Great Northern beans

1 teaspoon fresh or dried rosemary

1 teaspoon bottled crushed garlic

1/2 teaspoon celery seed

1/4 teaspoon red pepper flakes

1/4 teaspoon black pepper

1 15-ounce can ready-cut tomatoes

2 14-ounce cans chicken broth plus 1 can water OR 3 chicken bouillon cubes, 3 teaspoons chicken bouillon granules or 3 teaspoons chicken base plus 5 1/2 cups water

1/2 cup uncooked alphabet noodles, broken angel hair (vermicelli) pasta or spaghetti rigati (see Mom Tip 1)

Several handfuls fresh prewashed spinach or arugula (optional) (see Mom Tip 2)

Grated Parmesan cheese

Peel the carrots and onion and cut them into 1/2-inch pieces. Chop the prosciutto into 1/2-inch pieces.

Put the oil into a large pot and begin heating over medium-high heat. Add the carrots, onion and prosciutto and cook about 5 minutes, stirring occasionally, or until the vegetables begin to soften.

While the carrot mixture is cooking, drain the beans and rinse them under cold running water and then set aside.

Crush the rosemary using a mortar and pestle or break or cut into as small pieces as possible. Add it to the carrot mixture, along with the garlic, celery seed, red pepper flakes and black pepper and stir. Add the beans, tomatoes and their juice, chicken broth and water and bring to a boil over high heat.

Add the noodles and stir. Turn down to medium heat, cover and cook about 5 minutes, or until the noodles are ready. Stir in the spinach or arugula, if using, for a few seconds until it wilts. Serve immediately with Parmesan cheese sprinkled over top. Or set aside until ready to eat, and then reheat briefly.

Mom Tip 1: Spaghetti rigati, a new pasta with ridges introduced by Barilla, cooks in 6 minutes.

Mom Tip 2: Arugula is a salad green sold loose or in prewashed bags. It has a sharp, bitter flavor.

Polish Sausage Soup

Serves: 4 ✳

Preparation time: 10 minutes ✳

Cooking time: 10 minutes ✳

Time-saving tip: Use frozen chopped onions. ✳

I associate Kielbasa mostly with backyard barbecues and football games. It's a pretty macho food—the polar opposite of "fruit smoothies," which, while tasty, are decidedly unmacho. In fact, a lot of guys who eat Kielbasa would find it hard to even say the words "fruit smoothie."

This soup finds a middle ground. While it's got the slices of sausage, it's also got the more refined flavors of mushrooms, dill and garlic. It goes well with either a cold brewski or a mango smoothie.

    1 large onion

    1 tablespoon olive or corn oil

    1/2 pound precooked Kielbasa

    1 pound presliced mushrooms

    1 teaspoon bottled crushed garlic

    1/2 teaspoon dried dill

    1/4 teaspoon black pepper

2 14-ounce cans chicken broth OR 3 chicken bouillon cubes, 3 teaspoons chicken
   bouillon granules or 3 teaspoons chicken base plus 3 1/2 cups water

1 cup sauerkraut (see Mom Tip)

3/4 cup instant potato flakes plus more if needed

Peel the onion and cut it into 1/2-inch pieces. Put the oil into a large pot and begin heating over medium-high heat. Add the onion and cook about 5 minutes, stirring occasionally, or until it begins to soften.

While the onion is cooking, slice the Kielbasa into 1/4-inch slices and then set aside.

When the onion has begun to soften, add the mushrooms, garlic, dill and black pepper and cook another 2 minutes, or until the mushrooms begin to soften. Add the chicken broth and bring the mixture to a boil over high heat.

Drain and rinse the sauerkraut under cold running water to remove excess salt and add it to the pot. Add the instant potato flakes and stir until the mixture thickens slightly. Add the Kielbasa and heat 1 minute more. If the soup seems too thin for your taste, add a few more tablespoons instant potato flakes. If the soup seems too thick, add a few tablespoons water. Serve immediately. Or set aside until ready to eat, and then reheat briefly.

Mom Tip: Sauerkraut, which is basically pickled cabbage, is available in jars and cans and is usually stocked with other canned vegetables.

Salads

These aren't "Oh, I'll just have a salad"-type salads. These are "I'm starving. I think I'll have a salad!"-type salads. With substantial mixtures like Chicken Caesar Salad, Greek Salad with Shrimp and Taco Salad, you'll never again be happy with what the salad bar has to offer.

Calamari Salad

Chicken Caesar Salad

Greek Salad with Shrimp

Instant Dinner Salad

Taco Salad

Thai Pork Salad

Tuna, Artichoke and White Bean Salad

Calamari Salad

Serves: 4 ✳

Preparation time: 15 minutes ✳

Cooking time: 2–3 minutes ✳

Time-saving tip: Start boiling the water as soon as you enter the kitchen. ✳

Like most kids, I used to think of squid as bizarre, magical beasts who lived only in fairy tales and attacked submarines in Jules Verne novels. Well, it turns out they do exist and you can eat them. They're pretty good, too, although the cleaning and chopping part is not for the weak-hearted. Luckily they're frequently available precut.

I doubt Captain Nemo would have stocked red wine vinegar and crushed garlic on board the *Nautilus*, but if he had, he would have loved this salad.

2 pounds frozen, cleaned calamari (see Mom Tip 1)

1 teaspoon bottled lemon juice

1/4 cup olive oil

2 tablespoons red wine vinegar

1 teaspoon bottled crushed garlic

1 teaspoon dried oregano

1/2 teaspoon salt

1/2 teaspoon black pepper

4 large stalks celery

1/2 small red onion (about 1/4 cup)

1 15-ounce can cannellini or other white beans

Half-fill a medium pot with water, cover and begin heating over high heat.

If the calamari is already cleaned and cut into rings and tentacles, move on to the next step. If not, prepare the calamari (see Mom Tip 2), which will take about 20 minutes.

When the water comes to a boil, add the frozen calamari and lemon juice and cook for 2 minutes, or just until the rings and tentacles become opaque. If you cook it too long, it will taste like rubber bands. Drain the calamari, rinse it under cold running water and then set aside.

Put the olive oil, vinegar, garlic, oregano, salt and black pepper into a medium bowl and mix well.

Rinse and trim the celery and cut it into 1/4-inch pieces. Peel the red onion and cut it into 1/4-inch pieces. Add the vegetables to the bowl. Then add the calamari and mix well.

Drain and rinse the beans under cold running water. Add them to the bowl and mix well. Serve immediately or refrigerate, covered, until needed.

Mom Tip 1: Calamari, which is the Italian word for squid, is available in some super-markets and specialty food stores frozen and already cleaned. It most likely will have already been cut into thin rings and tentacles. If you are making this salad with fresh calamari, see Mom Tip 2.

Mom Tip 2: Calamari is also available fresh at some fish counters. Choose very small (about 4-inch-long) calamari. If it has not been cleaned, here's how to clean it: pull the tentacle section away from the V-shaped long tube. Keep the actual tentacles and about 1/2-inch of the ring they are attached to, but discard the rest. Then, holding the V-shaped tube in one hand, squeeze out and discard the white gelatinous material inside. Reach in and pull out and then discard the long plastic-like backbone. Cut the tentacles into 1-inch pieces. Cut the tube into 1/4-inch rings. Cook about 30 seconds in boiling water as described above.

Chicken Caesar Salad

Serves: 3–4 ✳

Preparation time: 15 minutes ✳

Cooking time: 8 minutes ✳

Time-saving tip: Use thickly sliced deli turkey or chicken instead of cooking the chicken. ✳

Unlike my dad, who can eat a head of iceberg lettuce like an apple, I find simple salads pretty boring. Chicken Caesar Salad is different. It's full of variety and is quite filling. Anchovies are still an unacquired taste for many, but they're hidden in the dressing so no one has to know they're there.

3 boneless chicken breast halves (about 1 1/4 pounds)

1 tablespoon olive or corn oil plus more if needed

2 10-ounce bags precut romaine lettuce

Bottled Caesar Dressing (see Mom Tip)

2 cups croutons

Slice each chicken breast crosswise into 3 thin slices. Put 1 tablespoon of the oil into a large frying pan or grill pan with ridges and begin heating over high heat. Cook as many of the chicken breast pieces as will fit into the pan about 2 minutes per side, or until both sides have turned white.

Test a piece by cutting into it to make sure the middle is white, not pink. Transfer the chicken to a plate and repeat until all the chicken is cooked, adding more oil if necessary. Cut the cooked chicken into pieces 1/2 inch wide and 1 inch long.

Put the lettuce into a large salad bowl and add the chicken pieces. Pour some dressing onto the salad and toss. To prevent the croutons from getting soggy, add them to the salad and toss just before serving. Offer extra dressing on the side.

Mom Tip: If you want to make your own dressing, here's how:

4 anchovy fillets
1/2 cup olive or corn oil
1/3 cup grated Parmesan cheese
3 tablespoons bottled lemon juice
1 tablespoon Dijon mustard
1 teaspoon bottled crushed garlic
1/2 teaspoon salt
1/4 teaspoon black pepper

Put all ingredients into a mini food processor or blender and process until smooth.

Greek Salad with Shrimp

Serves: 4 ✳

Preparation time: 20 minutes ✳

Cooking time: none ✳

Time-saving tip: Use cherry tomatoes. ✳

Is it really customary in Greece to smash plates after a meal, or is it just done in movies? It seems like an unusual pastime to me. My wife and I have wooden salad bowls that probably wouldn't smash no matter how hard we threw them. We could light them on fire, but that might not be as festive.

This is a basic Greek salad recipe. Some recipes ask for cucumber or red pepper, but we think we've hit all the high points without requiring extra chopping. The addition of shrimp bulks up the salad.

2 large or 4 small tomatoes

1/2 small red onion (about 1/4 cup)

2 10-ounce bags precut romaine lettuce

1 4-ounce package crumbled feta cheese

1 pound cooked small or medium shrimp

12 kalamata olives (optional) (see Mom Tip)

1/4 cup olive oil

2 tablespoons red wine vinegar

1 tablespoon bottled lemon juice

1 teaspoon bottled crushed garlic

1 teaspoon dried oregano

1 teaspoon salt

1/2 teaspoon dried dill

1/2 teaspoon black pepper

Rinse the tomatoes and cut them into bite-size pieces. Peel the red onion and cut it into 1/2-inch pieces. Put the lettuce, tomatoes and onion into a large salad bowl. Add the feta cheese, shrimp and olives, if using.

Put the oil, vinegar, lemon juice, garlic, oregano, salt, dill and black pepper into a small bottle. Cover with a lid and shake well. Pour over the salad, toss and serve immediately.

Mom Tip: Kalamata olives are black and come from Greece. They are available in cans or at some deli counters. They have a stronger, saltier flavor than American-style olives.

Instant Dinner Salad

Serves: 4–6 ✳

Preparation time: 20 minutes ✳

Cooking time: none ✳

Time-saving tip: Use a food processor to chop the carrots, celery, cucumber and onion. ✳

Everybody needs a recipe that clears out the veggie drawer. This salad has the variety and the volume to serve as dinner by itself. I don't know if you should use your big fork or salad fork. Considering the size of this salad, probably both.

2 medium carrots

2 medium stalks celery

2 medium tomatoes

1 cucumber

1/2 small red onion (about 1/4 cup)

1 15-ounce can beans (black, white, red, kidney or garbanzo)

1 cup leftover cooked rice or other cooked grain (see Mom Tip 1)

3 1/2 ounces roasted red peppers (about 8 peppers) (see Mom Tip 2)

1/4 cup balsamic vinegar

1/4 cup olive or corn oil

1/2 teaspoon bottled crushed garlic

1/2 teaspoon salt

1/4 teaspoon black pepper

3 tablespoons pine nuts

1 tablespoon bottled lemon juice (optional)

Rinse or peel the carrots, celery, tomatoes, cucumber and red onion and cut them into 1/4-inch pieces. Put them into a large salad bowl.

Drain the beans and rinse them under cold running water. Add to the bowl. Add the leftover rice or other cooked grain and set aside.

To make the dressing, rinse the red peppers under cold running water and finely chop them, removing and discarding any stems or seeds. Transfer them to a small bowl or an empty jar with a lid. Add the vinegar, oil, garlic, salt and black pepper and beat with a fork or shake. Pour the dressing over the salad. Sprinkle the pine nuts and lemon juice, if using, on top. Serve immediately or refrigerate, covered, until needed.

Mom Tip 1: *Couscous is the fastest grain to cook if you're starting from scratch. It takes 5 minutes.*

Mom Tip 2: *Kathy McCullough, who gave me this recipe, says these red peppers, sometimes labeled as pimientos, add a kick to the salad. You can find them in the canned or gourmet vegetable aisles at the grocery store.*

Taco Salad

Serves: 3–4 *

Preparation time: 15 minutes *

Cooking time: 6 minutes *

Time-saving tip: Use a 10-ounce bag precut lettuce. *

Eating tacos brings out all the worst aspects of my manners. If I'd eaten them on the first date with my wife, my life might have turned out differently. But, luckily for me, we ate Italian that night. It was much later when she first witnessed my Neanderthal approach to a taco, and by then she was prepared to forgive me. By combining the elements of a taco into a salad, you have all of the good taste, and none of the difficulty in assembly. And you avoid the inevitable disassembly that occurs when you bite into a standard taco.

1/2 pound ground turkey or beef

1/2 1-ounce envelope taco seasoning

1 large tomato

1 avocado

1/2 head iceberg lettuce

1/2 small red onion (about 1/4 cup)

1 15-ounce can black or kidney beans

1 4-ounce can sliced black olives (optional)

1 cup grated cheddar or Monterey Jack cheese

Bottled vinaigrette dressing

1 to 2 cups corn chips

Put the ground meat into a non-stick frying pan and cook about 5 minutes over medium heat, stirring occasionally, or until it browns. Drain and discard the fat. Add the taco seasoning and cook over medium heat for 1 minute, stirring so that the spice mixture clings to the meat. Remove from heat and then set aside.

Rinse the tomato and cut it into 1/2-inch pieces. Cut the avocado in half, remove and discard the pit and then remove the peel. Cut it into 1/2-inch cubes. Rinse the lettuce and cut it into 1-inch pieces. Peel the red onion and cut it into 1/4-inch pieces. Put the tomato, avocado, lettuce and red onion into a large salad bowl.

Drain the beans, rinse them under cold running water and add them to the bowl. Drain the olives, if using, and add them to the bowl. Add the cooked ground meat and the cheese and toss to combine. Just before serving, add the salad dressing and corn chips and toss again. The corn chips will get soggy if they sit in the salad for any length of time.

Thai Pork Salad

Serves: 4 ✳
Preparation time: 20 minutes ✳
Cooking time: 5 minutes ✳
Time-saving tip: Buy pork already cut into thin strips. ✳

Thai Pork Salad uses ingredients that you probably keep on hand to make a great Thai taste. It's easy to make, and it uses my favorite cooking tool: the wok. The wok, to me, is like an old-fashioned microwave. The pork strips in this recipe cook in 2 minutes. That's faster than it takes to clean up. The only other labor involved here is putting things in bowls.

1 pound boneless pork chops or tenderloin

2 tablespoons brown sugar

2 tablespoons bottled lime juice

1 tablespoon ketchup

1 tablespoon soy sauce

1 teaspoon bottled crushed garlic

1/8 teaspoon cayenne pepper or more if you like really spicy food

6 scallions

1 16-ounce bag shredded cabbage or coleslaw mixture

1 tablespoon peanut or corn oil

1/2 cup dry roasted peanuts or more, if desired

Handful bean sprouts (optional)

Cut the pork into strips about 1 inch long, 1/8 inch wide and 1/8 inch thick.

Put the brown sugar, lime juice, ketchup, soy sauce, garlic and cayenne pepper into a medium bowl and mix well. Add the pork strips and mix and then set aside to marinate for 10 minutes.

Rinse and trim the scallions and then cut them into 1-inch pieces.

Put the cabbage into a large serving bowl. Add the scallion pieces and then set aside.

Put the oil into a large frying pan or wok and begin heating over medium-high heat. With a slotted spoon, lift the pork strips from the marinade and add them to the pan. Stir-fry about 1 minute, or until the strips are no longer pink. Add the marinade to the pan and bring the mixture to a boil. Cook 1 minute more.

Remove from heat and pour the contents of the pan over the cabbage mixture. Add the peanuts and bean sprouts, if using, and toss the salad. Serve immediately.

Tuna, Artichoke and White Bean Salad

Serves: 4 ✳

Preparation time: 20 minutes ✳

Cooking time: none ✳

Time-saving tip: Use a mini food processor to chop the parsley or cilantro. ✳

This may seem like an odd combination, but there may also have been a time when mixing lettuce, tomato and cucumber would have been considered madness. So, go ahead and try Tuna, Artichoke and White Bean Salad. It's the salad of the future.

4 scallions

2 large stalks celery

1/2 medium jicama (see Mom Tip 1)

1/2 cup fresh parsley or cilantro

2 15-ounce cans cannellini or other white beans

1 14-ounce can artichoke hearts

1 cup black olives (optional)

2 6-ounce cans imported tuna in olive oil (see Mom Tip 2)

1/4 cup lemon juice

1/2 teaspoon dried dill

1/2 teaspoon salt

1/4 teaspoon black pepper

Rinse and trim the scallions and celery and then cut them into 1/2-inch pieces. Peel the jicama and cut it into 1/2-inch cubes. Rinse the parsley or cilantro. Cut off and discard the stems and cut the leafy parts into 1/2-inch pieces. Put the vegetables into a large salad bowl.

Drain and rinse the beans under cold running water. Drain the artichoke hearts and cut them into eighths. Add the beans, artichoke hearts and olives, if using, to the bowl.

Drain the tuna and put the oil into a cup. Add the tuna to the bowl and separate into chunks. Add the lemon juice, dill, salt and black pepper to the oil in the cup and mix well. Pour the dressing over the tuna mixture and toss gently. Serve immediately or refrigerate, covered, until needed.

Mom Tip 1: Jicama is a root vegetable that, when peeled, sliced and eaten raw, looks and tastes somewhat like a water chestnut. Small jicamas are about the size of a baseball and have a brown skin. Store them in the vegetable compartment of the refrigerator and slice as needed. They last about a week.

Mom Tip 2: Canned imported tuna, which is available in gourmet food shops and some large grocery stores, has more flavor than regular canned tuna. If you prefer to use tuna packed in water, drain it and add 1/4 cup olive oil when you add the lemon juice.

Sandwiches & Tortillas

Things have changed since the Earl of Sandwich first invented the food that bears his name. I doubt the Earl would have thought of such combinations as Black Bean Wraps, Philly Cheese Steak Sandwiches or Shrimp Tortillas. But it all goes back to him. So, thank you, Earl, for being too lazy to get up from the gaming table to go to the dinner table. Your slothfulness was the world's gain.

Black Bean Wraps

Fish Tacos

Lobster Rolls

Philly Cheese Steak Sandwiches

Reuben Bagels

Roasted Portobello Mushroom Burgers

Shrimp Tortillas

Black Bean Wraps

Serves: 4 (2 wraps per person) ✳

Preparation time: 15 minutes ✳

Cooking time: 4 minutes ✳

Time-saving tip: Use cilantro-flavored olive oil and skip the cilantro. ✳

Black Bean Wraps may sound like a new-age facial treatment (and if it removed blemishes, I'm sure people would use it, even if it left them smelling like a burrito). But they're actually quick, homemade soft tacos. The ingredients are flexible, depending on what you have available. But if you serve them without the black beans, the name will be hard to justify.

3 scallions

1 large red bell pepper

1/2 cup fresh cilantro

2 15-ounce cans black beans

1 15-ounce can whole-kernel corn

1 4-ounce can diced green chiles

3 tablespoons olive or corn oil

2 tablespoons red wine vinegar

1/2 teaspoon salt

1/2 teaspoon garlic powder

1/4 teaspoon black pepper

8 8-inch flour tortillas

Grated cheddar cheese (optional)

Hot pepper sauce or Tabasco Chipotle Pepper Sauce (optional)

Rinse and trim the scallions and cut them into 1/4-inch pieces. Rinse the bell pepper, cut it in half, remove and discard the stem and seeds and then cut it into 1/4-inch pieces. Rinse and pat dry the cilantro. Cut off and discard the stems and cut the leafy parts into 1/2-inch pieces. Drain the beans and rinse them under cold running water. Drain the corn and green chiles.

Put the scallions, bell pepper, cilantro, beans, corn and green chiles into a large bowl. Add the oil, vinegar, salt, garlic powder and black pepper and mix well and then set aside.

Remove the tortillas from their package, wrap them in a tea towel or paper towel and microwave on high for 1 minute. Transfer the tortillas to a serving plate. Spoon 1/2 to 2/3 cup of the bean mixture into the center of each tortilla. Sprinkle with cheddar cheese and hot pepper sauce, if using. Wrap each tortilla, folding it at the bottom so the filling doesn't fall out when it's held upright. Serve immediately.

Fish Tacos

Serves: 4 ✳

Preparation time: 10 minutes ✳

Cooking time: 8–10 minutes ✳

Time-saving tip: Use packaged coleslaw mix. ✳

I'd never heard of fish tacos until about five years ago. All of a sudden they were available all over the place, challenging chicken and beef for taco supremacy. It was a food trend that I immediately liked. We're too late to be trendy, but here's our addition to the fish taco pantheon. My favorite touch is the avocado.

4 scallions or 1/2 small red onion

1 ripe avocado

2 cups shredded cabbage or lettuce

Salsa

1 1/2 pounds catfish fillets (see Mom Tip)

3 tablespoons flour

1/2 teaspoon salt

1/4 teaspoon black pepper

3 tablespoons olive or corn oil

8 8-inch flour tortillas or 12 5-inch corn tortillas

Lime wedges

Rinse and trim the scallions and cut them into 1/4-inch pieces. Or if you are using red onion, peel it and cut it into 1/4-inch pieces. Put the scallions or onion into a small serving bowl and then set aside. Cut the avocado in half, remove and discard the pit and then remove the peel. Slice thinly and put the slices into another small serving bowl. Put the cabbage or lettuce into a third bowl and the salsa into a fourth. Set them on the table.

Rinse the catfish fillets and remove any visible bones. There shouldn't be many, if any. Cut the fillets into 1-inch pieces. Put the flour, salt and black pepper into a plastic or paper bag and add the catfish pieces. Close the bag tightly and gently shake until all the fish surfaces are covered with the flour mixture.

Put the oil into a large frying pan or wok and begin heating over medium-high heat. Add the catfish pieces. Cook for 8–10 minutes, stirring occasionally, or until the pieces have begun to brown and the catfish is white throughout. Test a piece to make sure it's done. Remove from heat and cover to keep warm.

Remove the tortillas from their package, wrap them in a tea towel or paper towel and microwave on high for 1 minute. Transfer the tortillas to a serving plate. Diners can fill their own tortillas with fish, scallions or onion, avocado, cabbage or lettuce and salsa. Serve with lime wedges and plenty of napkins.

Mom Tip: Catfish is a firm white fish that will hold its shape when cooked. You can substitute cod, red snapper or tilapia.

Lobster Rolls

Serves: 4

Preparation time: 20 minutes

Cooking time: 2 minutes

Time-saving tip: Don't heat the buns.

If you can get your hands on some real lobster at a reasonable price, go for it. If not, don't be afraid of the term "imitation crab." I know it conjures up images of such infomercial fare as "Diamonoids" and "Genuine Faux Pearls," but "imitation crab" is still seafood. It tastes good on its own merits—not because when you close your eyes you can imagine you're eating something else.

"Lobster Rolls" are traditionally served on hotdog buns, a vestige of the recipe's humble beginnings before lobster was the delicacy it is today. Hotdog buns still serve this recipe well, as their very blandness allows the filling to dominate. But feel free to upgrade to rolls more to your taste.

1 pound (about 2 cups) cooked lobster meat or imitation crab (Surimi, see page 13)

2 medium stalks celery

1/4 cup mayonnaise

2 tablespoons bottled lemon juice

8 hotdog buns (see Mom Tip)

1 tablespoon butter

Cut the lobster or crab into 1/2-inch pieces. Rinse and trim the celery and cut it into 1/4-inch slices.

Put the lobster or crab, celery, mayonnaise and lemon juice into a large bowl and mix lightly. If the mixture seems too dry, add 1 to 2 tablespoons water.

If the buns are not already precut, cut each one down the middle of the top, being careful not to cut through the whole way. If the buns are already precut, plan to serve them with the cut side facing up.

Melt the butter in a large frying pan over medium-high heat and place 4 buns, cut side down, in the pan. Press down with a spatula and fry the buns about 30 seconds, or until lightly browned. Turn them over and brown the other side. Repeat with the other 4 buns when you're ready to serve seconds.

Heap 1/8 of the seafood mixture into each bun and serve immediately.

Mom Tip: Traditional lobster roll buns are cut down the middle of the top, rather than the normal cut through the side. My sister-in-law Sue Hagen, who lives on the New Hampshire coast, makes her own rolls so she can make the cut herself. But that step gets in the way of fast cooking.

Philly Cheese Steak Sandwiches

Serves: 4 ✳

Preparation time: 10–12 minutes ✳

Cooking time: 12 minutes ✳

Time-saving tip: Use leftover roast beef or deli roast beef. ✳

I've only been to Philadelphia once, but I was there long enough to buy a cheese steak from a street vendor. It was terrific. In my opinion, it ranks right up there with the U.S. Constitution as an important Philadelphia contribution to the American landscape. I hope our sandwiches live up to street vendor standards.

4 6-inch-long rolls

1 medium onion

1 medium green bell pepper (optional)

2 tablespoons olive or corn oil

1/2 pound presliced mushrooms (optional)

1/2 teaspoon salt

1/4 teaspoon black pepper

1 pound sirloin steak or leftover roast beef

1 cup grated mozzarella, American or provolone cheese

Place an oven rack in the middle position and preheat the oven to 350 degrees F. Slice the rolls three-quarters through and place them on a baking sheet and then set aside.

Peel and thinly slice the onion. Rinse the bell pepper, if using, cut it in half, remove and discard the stem and seeds and cut it into 1/2-inch pieces. Put the oil into a large frying pan and begin heating over medium-high heat. Add the onion, bell pepper, if using, mushrooms, if using, salt and black pepper and cook about 10 minutes, stirring occasionally, or until the vegetables are very soft. After they have cooked 5 minutes, put the rolls into the oven to heat.

Slice the steak or roast beef into paper-thin slices and add to the vegetable mixture. If using raw steak, cook about 1 minute per side, or until it's no longer red. If using leftover roast beef, no additional cooking is necessary. Simply stir the mixture.

Remove the rolls from the oven and fill each with 1/4 of the meat mixture. Add 1/4 of the cheese to each roll and return the rolls to the oven. Heat about 2 minutes, or until the cheese melts. Serve immediately.

Reuben Bagels

Serves: 4 ✳

Preparation time: 12 minutes ✳

Cooking time: 9–13 minutes ✳

Time-saving tip: Use leftover chicken or 1/4 inch thick sliced deli chicken, turkey, corned beef or pastrami. ✳

Typically a Reuben sandwich contains corned beef or pastrami. Those are both good, but hired goons from the Carnegie Deli won't break down your door and smash your dinnerware if you use chicken instead. I prefer chicken. And we've made some other modifications, including replacing the bread with bagels, which are more substantial and keep the sandwich together better. In your own kitchen, you can make things your own way.

2 boneless chicken breast halves (about 1 pound)

1 tablespoon olive oil plus more if needed

3 tablespoons ketchup

3 tablespoons mayonnaise

1 tablespoon sweet relish

4 pumpernickel or rye bagels, halved

4 slices Swiss cheese

1/2 cup sauerkraut (see Mom Tip 1)

Slice the uncooked chicken breasts into 1/4-inch slices. Put 1 tablespoon of the oil into a large frying pan or grill pan with ridges and begin heating over high heat. Cook as many of the chicken pieces as will fit into the pan about 2 minutes per side, or until both sides have turned white. Test a piece by cutting into it to make sure the middle is white, not pink. Transfer the chicken to a plate and repeat until all the chicken is cooked, adding more oil if necessary.

Put the ketchup, mayonnaise and relish into a small bowl and mix well.

Lay 4 bagel halves in a large ungreased frying pan or griddle, cut side up. Spread about 1 teaspoon of the ketchup mixture on the top of each. Lay a slice of chicken over that, and then a slice of cheese. Cover the cheese with 2 tablespoons sauerkraut. Add another slice of chicken. Spread the rest of the ketchup mixture equally over the chicken and top with a bagel half.

Cover the frying pan or griddle with a deep lid (see Mom Tip 2) and turn down to medium heat. Cook about 3 minutes, or until the bottom of the bagels begin to brown. Remove the lid, carefully turn the bagels over so that the filling doesn't fall out. Put the lid back and cook another 2 minutes, or until the cheese melts. Serve immediately.

Mom Tip 1: Sauerkraut, which is basically pickled cabbage, is available in jars and cans and is usually stocked with other canned vegetables.

Mom Tip 2: A deep lid allows the bagel to be fully enclosed, thus letting the filling get hot while the bottom of the bagel browns. If you don't have a deep lid, use a large pot instead, turning it upside down and placing it over the frying pan or griddle.

Roasted Portobello Mushroom Burgers

Serves: 4 ✳

Preparation time: 10 minutes ✳

Cooking time: 15 minutes ✳

Time-saving tip: Use vegetable oil spray instead of oil to coat the mushrooms. ✳

Portobello mushrooms are the biggest mushrooms I've ever seen. You could stick a straw in one and use it as a parasol. Because they're round and filling, mom started making these as hamburger substitutes for stray vegetarians at her regular barbecues. My wife always wants at least two. To her, the Fourth of July means freedom, liberty and Roasted Portobello Mushroom Burgers. This recipe is adapted for the oven, so you can make them year-round.

4 large portobello mushrooms

3 tablespoons mayonnaise

1 teaspoon bottled crushed garlic

1/2 teaspoon salt

1/4 teaspoon black pepper

2 teaspoons olive or corn oil

4 hamburger buns

Place one of the oven racks in the middle position and preheat the oven to 450 degrees F. Line a baking sheet with aluminum foil for easy cleanup.

Rinse the smooth side of the mushrooms, wiping away any dirt, and pat them dry with a paper towel. Loosen each stem by pushing and pulling gently so that you don't break the mushrooms in half. Pull the stems away from the mushrooms. Cut away and discard the bottom 1/4 inch of the stems. Rinse the remaining stems, chop them into 1/8-inch pieces and then set aside.

Put the mayonnaise, garlic, salt and black pepper into a small bowl and stir in the pieces of chopped stem.

Spread 1/2 teaspoon of the oil on the smooth side of each mushroom and place them on the baking sheet, smooth side down. This is to prevent the mushrooms from sticking. Spoon 1/4 of the mushroom mixture into the cavity of each mushroom and spread it around. Bake uncovered for 15 minutes, or until the mushrooms have softened and slightly shrunk. About 3 minutes before serving, put the hamburger buns into the oven to heat. When the mushrooms are ready and the buns are hot, transfer the mushrooms to the buns and serve immediately.

Shrimp Tortillas

Serves: 4 ✳

Preparation time: 5 minutes ✳

Cooking time: 8 minutes ✳

Time-saving tip: Use two frying pans so you can cook more at once. ✳

At dinnertime, I'm generally pretty adventurous. Octopus, Ostrich Burgers, Eel Pie, bring 'em on. But for lunch I'm a creature of habit. I'm frequently either in a rush or feeling lazy, so I'll usually settle for a tuna sandwich or a bagel. That's why recipes like this one are so perfect. Shrimp Tortillas take around 10 minutes to make and are miles away from the same old thing.

2 scallions

2 ripe avocados

8 8-inch flour tortillas

1 pound cooked, peeled shrimp

2 cups (8 ounces) grated mozzarella cheese

Salsa (optional)

Rinse and trim the scallions and cut them into 1/4-inch pieces. Cut the avocados in half, remove and discard the pits and then remove the peel. Slice thinly.

Place 1 tortilla in a dry frying pan and heat over medium-high heat for a few seconds. Turn the tortilla over and quickly cover with 1/8 of the scallions, avocado slices, shrimp and cheese. Cover with a lid and cook over medium-high heat for 30–45 seconds, or until the cheese melts. Be careful that the tortilla doesn't get overly crisp. Remove the lid and fold the tortilla in half so that it looks like a half-moon. Serve immediately with salsa, if using. Repeat the process until all the tortillas are cooked.

Eggs & Cheese

I love restaurants that serve breakfast at all hours of the day. There's something delightfully upside down about having eggs for dinner. From classic Omelets to the more modern Mushroom and Zucchini Frittata and Chile Rellenos Mini Casseroles, there are now some great options for eggheads like me.

I also love big, cheesy foods. Cheese Bread Bowls and Welsh Rarebit are treats, and I recommend that you try Grilled Halloumi Cheese Kebabs.

Cheese Bread Bowl

Chile Rellenos Mini Casseroles

Grilled Halloumi Cheese Kebabs

Mushroom and Zucchini Frittata

Omelets

Welsh Rarebit

Cheese Bread Bowl

Serves: 4 ✳

Preparation time: 10 minutes ✳

Cooking time: 10 minutes ✳

Time-saving tip: Start with the cheese at room temperature, if possible. It will melt faster. ✳

The Cheese Bread Bowl was born as an appetizer, but it grew up to be a main course. While it's the ultimate version of cheese and crackers, it's so filling that you won't have room for anything else if you eat it first. This is one time when it's okay to fill up on bread.

   1 loaf baguette-style French bread or unsliced round loaf

   3 tablespoons melted butter or olive oil

   1 teaspoon bottled crushed garlic

   3/4 pound brie cheese (see Mom Tip)

Place one of the oven racks in the middle position and preheat the oven to 375 degrees F.

If using French bread, cut it into 4 equal lengths and treat each one as a small "bowl." Or use a round loaf.

Slice the top inch off the bread and then set aside to use as a "lid." Carefully cut out the inside of the bread, leaving at least 1/2 inch of crust to serve as the bowl. Cut the bread you've removed into 1-inch cubes and then set aside.

Mix the butter or olive oil and garlic in a small container. Spoon it into the bread bowl(s) and spread it around.

Place the bread bowl(s) and lid(s) on a baking sheet and bake for 10 minutes.

While the bread is heating, trim and discard the white skin on the brie. Cut the cheese into 1-inch pieces, and then put them into a small frying pan and begin heating over medium heat. Stir constantly about 5 minutes, or until cheese is melted.

Remove the bread bowl(s) from the oven and transfer the melted cheese to the bowl(s). Place the bowl(s) on a serving tray, put on the lid(s) and pile the bread pieces around the bowl(s). Serve immediately. Dip the bread pieces into the cheese. When the bread is used up, break off pieces of the bowl and continue eating. If using bowls made of French bread, give each person a bowl.

Mom Tip: If you don't like brie, substitute muenster, Monterey Jack or cheddar cheese.

Chile Rellenos Mini Casseroles

Serves: 4 ✳

Preparation time: 10 minutes ✳

Cooking time: 15 minutes ✳

Time-saving tip: Bake the mixture in 12 ramekins rather than 8. With less liquid in each ramekin, it will cook more quickly. ✳

I love casseroles. The bigger and cheesier and the more ingredients the better. Unfortunately they usually take forever to cook. This recipe, however, has a clever trick. By dividing the casserole into smaller baking dishes you can really speed up the process. Chile Rellenos Mini Casseroles taste like thick, filling, Mexican scrambled eggs.

1 tablespoon olive or corn oil

2 4-ounce cans diced green chiles (see Mom Tip)

1 cup (4 ounces) grated Monterey Jack cheese

1 cup (4 ounces) grated cheddar cheese

2 5-ounce cans evaporated milk

6 large eggs

1/2 teaspoon salt

1/4 teaspoon black pepper

Salsa (optional)

Place an oven rack in the middle position and preheat the oven to 400 degrees F.

Wipe eight 6-ounce ovenproof ramekins or ovenproof coffee cups with a bit of oil and place on a baking sheet.

Drain the green chiles, discarding the liquid, and divide them equally among the ramekins or cups. Top each with 2 tablespoons Monterey Jack cheese and 2 tablespoons cheddar cheese.

Put the evaporated milk, eggs, salt and black pepper into a medium bowl and mix well. Pour the mixture over the cheese, dividing it equally.

Transfer the ramekins or cups to the oven on the baking sheet and bake about 15 minutes, or until the cheese mixture is firm and the top is just beginning to brown. Serve immediately with salsa, if using.

Mom Tip: Make sure you buy mild green chiles rather than jalapeño peppers, which may look the same but are much hotter.

Grilled Halloumi Cheese Kebabs

Serves: 2–3 ✳

Preparation time: 15 minutes ✳

Cooking time: 6 minutes ✳

Time-saving tip: Use croutons instead of the roll, but instead of threading them on the skewers, just serve them on the side. ✳

It's strange to be over 30 and discover a food you've never heard of. Halloumi cheese, which my mom introduced to me shortly after a friend introduced it to her, is a solid, filling cheese from Cyprus that works really well on kebabs. It makes me wonder what other culinary secrets the world is keeping.

Olive oil

9 ounces Halloumi cheese (see Mom Tip 1)

1 small red or yellow bell pepper

1 small zucchini

1 6-inch-long roll

18 cherry tomatoes

Wooden skewers (see Mom Tip 2)

Preheat the broiler. Make sure the top oven rack is in the highest position, just under the broiling unit. Wipe a baking sheet with a bit of oil and then set aside. Or use a nonstick sheet.

Cut the Halloumi cheese into 1-inch squares. Rinse the bell pepper, cut in half, remove and discard the stem and seeds and cut it into 1-inch pieces. Rinse and trim the ends of the zucchini and cut it into 1/4-inch slices. Cut the roll into 1-inch cubes. Rinse the cherry tomatoes.

Thread the tomatoes, pieces of cheese, bell pepper, zucchini and roll onto the wooden skewers, leaving no space between each piece. Place the skewers on the baking sheet and drizzle with oil. Broil for 2–3 minutes per side, or until the cheese begins to brown. It will not melt. Watch the kebabs carefully because the roll cubes may start to burn. Serve immediately.

Mom Tip 1: Halloumi cheese is usually sold in 9-ounce packages and is available in specialty food stores and through mail order at www.halloumicheese.com. Feta cheese is somewhat similar and may be substituted in this recipe, but it doesn't work as well because it is saltier and more crumbly.

Mom Tip 2: Use wooden skewers, rather than metal ones, because they are easier to push through the cheese without causing it to crumble.

Mom Tip 3: You can also pan-grill these kebabs. Put 2 tablespoons oil into a large frying pan, grill pan or griddle and begin heating over medium-high heat. Place the kebabs in the pan and cook about 4 minutes per side, or until the cheese turns golden brown. It will not melt. Serve immediately.

Mushroom and Zucchini Frittata

Serves: 4 ✳

Preparation time: 10 minutes ✳

Cooking time: 15 minutes ✳

Time-saving tip: Use frozen chopped onions and canned mushrooms and substitute roasted red peppers for the zucchini. ✳

Before I married a vegetarian, I'd never heard of such things as frittatas. I wasn't sure whether they were a female thing or a vegetarian thing. But I liked them. They tasted good, and they didn't have the fundamental flaw of much of the food my wife ate instead of meat, like being as filling as an appetizer. Mushroom and Zucchini Frittatas are as filling as dinner should be.

1 large onion

2 medium zucchini

2 tablespoons olive oil

1/2 pound presliced mushrooms

8 large eggs

1/4 cup grated Parmesan cheese or crumbled feta cheese

1/2 teaspoon salt

Dash black pepper

Preheat the broiler. Make sure the top oven rack is in the highest position, just under the broiling unit.

Peel the onion and cut it into 1/2-inch pieces. Rinse and trim the ends of the zucchini and cut into 1/4-inch slices.

Put the oil into a large ovenproof frying pan (see Mom Tip 1) and begin heating over medium-high heat. Add the onion and cook about 5 minutes, stirring occasionally, or until it begins to soften. Add the zucchini and mushrooms and cook 5 minutes more, or until the zucchini is soft and the mushrooms have begun to shrink.

While the vegetables cook, break the eggs in a bowl, add the Parmesan or feta cheese, salt and black pepper and beat until frothy. When the vegetables are cooked, pour the egg mixture over them and spread the vegetables around so they're at least partly covered with the egg mixture. Cover and turn down to low heat. Cook about 5 minutes and check to see if the eggs are set on the bottom. If not, cook another 2–3 minutes. The top will still be slightly runny. The cooking time depends partly on how big the frying pan is. Remove the lid and slide the frying pan under the broiler, with the handle sticking out and the broiler door open. Broil the eggs about 1 minute, or until the eggs finish cooking and begin to brown. Remove from oven and cut into 4 wedges. Serve immediately or set aside and serve warm.

Mom Tip 1: The size of the pan will determine how long the frittata will need to cook. The bigger the pan, the quicker the cooking. If you cut the recipe in half, cook the frittata in a 7-inch frying pan. The resulting frittata will be about 2 inches thick.

Mom Tip 2: If you want a more substantial dish, add 1 cup 1/4-inch diced potatoes when you add the onions. Instead of zucchini, you can use other cooked vegetables such as asparagus, green beans or artichoke hearts.

Omelets

Serves: 4 ✳

Preparation time: 1 minute ✳

Cooking time: About 2 minutes per omelet plus time to prepare filling, if needed ✳

Time-saving tip: Grated cheese is the quickest filling. ✳

I love the idea of having breakfast for dinner. As a college student that meant eating four bowls of Cocoa Pebbles. As an adult with responsibilities, it means an omelet with a little cheese, a few veggies and some slices of ham. And, at most, two bowls of Cocoa Pebbles. Omelets are a great emergency meal because you only really need eggs and maybe cheese, and most people keep those around.

8 large eggs

1/2 teaspoon salt

1/4 teaspoon black pepper

1 teaspoon olive or corn oil

4 teaspoons butter

FILLING (optional):

No more than 1/4 cup filling per omelet:

* thinly sliced mushrooms cooked for 3 minutes in 1 tablespoon butter

* grated cheddar, Monterey Jack or Parmesan cheese

* ham cut into 1/4-inch slivers

* leftover cooked vegetables

Read these directions several times before starting an omelet because it will cook so fast you won't have time to read them again.

The frying pan is the key. It should be about 7 inches wide at the bottom and have sloping sides so you can slide the omelet right out onto a plate. It is important that the omelet not stick to the pan while it is being cooked.

Break the eggs into a medium bowl and add the salt and black pepper. Mix lightly with a fork just until the white and yolk are combined (about 35 strokes).

If you're planning to put a filling inside each omelet, prepare it now.

Put the oil in the frying pan and begin heating over medium-high heat. Tip the pan so that the oil covers all the inner surfaces. When it starts to sizzle, anywhere from 20 seconds to 2 minutes, depending on the thickness of the pan, add 1 teaspoon of the butter. As soon as the butter melts and begins to froth, a matter of seconds, pour 1/4 cup of the egg mixture into the pan.

The eggs will begin to cook immediately. With one hand, shake the pan back and forth across the burner to keep the omelet from sticking, and with the other use a fork or metal spatula to lift the edge of the already cooked portion. This allows the uncooked liquid to run underneath. Tip the pan to speed this process. This all happens in about 30 seconds.

While the top of the omelet is still slightly runny, sprinkle on any filling. Then fold the omelet over on itself, using a fork or spatula, making a half-moon shape. If it won't fold, slide half of it onto the plate and fold the remaining half on top. Serve immediately.

Add 1 more teaspoon of the butter to the hot pan, and when it begins to froth make the next omelet. Repeat until all 4 omelets are cooked.

Mom Warning: Overcooking is the biggest problem with omelets. By the time they look done, they're probably overdone. Perfectly cooked omelets may seem very moist, but that's the way they're supposed to be.

Welsh Rarebit

Serves: 4 ✳

Preparation time: 10 minutes ✳

Cooking time: 7 minutes ✳

Time-saving tip: Skip toasting the bread. ✳

Some food names are very descriptive. "tuna fish sandwich," for instance. You know exactly what you're getting. The name "Welsh Rarebit" tells you nothing. To the uninitiated, it could be a garden tool. But it's actually melted cheese mixed with unique flavors and served on toast. It's perfect for when you need a good, filling lunch.

8 to 10 large slices good-quality bread

3/4 cup beer or milk

2 teaspoons Worcestershire sauce

1 teaspoon dry mustard

1/4 teaspoon salt

1/4 teaspoon black pepper

4 cups grated cheddar cheese

Place an oven rack in the middle position and preheat the oven to 450 degrees F.

If the bread is not sliced, slice it 3/4 inch thick. Lightly toast the bread (until it just begins to brown) and place the slices on a baking sheet. If they don't all fit, use a second sheet. Set aside.

Put the beer or milk, Worcestershire sauce, dry mustard, salt and black pepper into a large heavy-duty pot or frying pan and begin heating over medium-high heat. When it boils, turn down to medium-low heat and add the cheese. Stir continually about 1 minute, or until the cheese melts. Do not let the mixture boil. Remove from heat.

Spoon the cheese mixture onto the toast. Bake about 5 minutes, or until the cheese is bubbly. Transfer the toasts to plates and serve immediately.

Pasta

There are so many varieties of pasta these days. I seem to remember as a child (it wasn't that long ago, although it was in the last millennium) that my choices were lasagna, ravioli and spaghetti. Occasionally, when mom was feeling fancy, she'd make linguine. Now when I shop I'm confronted with a dizzying array of choices, from cappellini to rigatoni to bow ties. And there are so many options for sauces. We've narrowed it down to ten recipes, ranging from the classic Linguine with White Clam Sauce to the more unusual Penne with Indian-Style Cauliflower Sauce. But they're all good, and they all tell you exactly what to buy so you don't have to spend 20 minutes in the pasta aisle.

Angel Hair Pasta with Tomatoes and Basil

Basil and Scallop Linguine

Bow Tie Pasta with Hot Sausage Sauce

Fusilli with Asparagus and Artichoke Hearts

Linguine with White Clam Sauce

Pasta Carbonara

Penne with Indian-Style Cauliflower Sauce

Spaghetti with Olives and Capers

Spaghetti with Spicy Zucchini Sauce

Tortellini with Spinach and Goat Cheese

Angel Hair Pasta with Tomatoes and Basil

Serves: 4–6 ✳

Preparation time: 15 minutes ✳

Cooking time: 0 minutes for sauce plus 4–6 minutes for pasta ✳

Time-saving tip: Use fresh noodles, which cook in 1 minute. Because fresh noodles weigh more, you will need 1 1/2 pounds to serve 4 people. ✳

You'd be surprised how often my wife and I forget that dinnertime is approaching. Around 6 p.m. we'll look at each other and then at the drawer where we keep the takeout menus. But then we think better of it and choose one of our emergency meals. Angel Hair Pasta with Tomatoes and Basil is one of our favorites. It's quick and easy, and we usually have the ingredients on hand. And with a 15-minute prep time, we're sitting down to eat long before the delivery guy would have arrived.

1/2 small red onion (about 1/4 cup)

1/2 cup fresh basil or 1 teaspoon dried basil

1 teaspoon bottled crushed garlic

1 28-ounce can ready-cut tomatoes (see Mom Tip 1)

2 tablespoons olive oil

1/2 teaspoon salt

1/4 teaspoon black pepper

16 ounces angel hair (vermicelli) pasta

Grated Parmesan cheese (optional)

Fill a large pot with water, cover and begin heating over high heat.

Peel the red onion and cut it into 1/4-inch pieces. Rinse the fresh basil, if using, and cut it into thin strips.

Put the red onion and basil into a large bowl. Add the garlic. Drain the tomatoes and add to the bowl, discarding the liquid. Add the olive oil, salt and black pepper. Set the mixture aside.

When the water comes to a boil, add the angel hair pasta and cook according to directions.

Drain the pasta and transfer it to the bowl. Mix well and sprinkle with Parmesan cheese, if desired. Serve immediately or leave until the pasta reaches room temperature.

Mom Tip 1: Use 2 pounds fresh tomatoes for an even better taste. Ideally you would first remove the skins by dropping the tomatoes into boiling water for 30 seconds and then pulling off the skins. Then cut into 1/2-inch pieces.

Mom Tip 2: Add 1/2 cup toasted pine nuts and 1 to 2 cups 1/2-inch-cubed mozzarella cheese to vary the flavor.

Basil and Scallop Linguine

Serves: 4 ✳

Preparation time: 5 minutes ✳

Cooking time: 13 minutes for sauce plus 8 minutes for linguine
(sauce and linguine overlap cooking time) ✳

Time-saving tip: Use fresh noodles, which cook in 2–3 minutes. Because fresh noodles weigh more, you will need 1 1/2 pounds to serve 4 people. ✳

For decades the only spaghetti I wanted to eat had tomato sauce and ground beef. But like so many other habits, marriage "cured" me of this one too. My wife enjoys all different kinds of sauces, and she greatly expanded my horizons.

She grows fresh basil in the backyard, and it really enlivens this recipe. If she could raise scallops in the bathtub, she'd really be onto something.

1/4 cup fresh basil or 2 teaspoons dried basil

1 15-ounce can ready-cut tomatoes

1/2 cup dry white wine

2 tablespoons tomato paste

1 teaspoon bottled crushed garlic

1/4 teaspoon red pepper flakes

2 scallions

16 ounces linguine

1 pound small raw scallops (see Mom Tip)

Fill a large pot with water, cover and begin heating over high heat.

While the water is heating, rinse the fresh basil, if using, and cut it into thin strips. Put the basil, tomatoes and their juice, white wine, tomato paste, garlic and red pepper flakes into a pot large enough to hold a pound of cooked linguine. Bring the mixture to a boil over medium-high heat, turn down to medium heat and cook, uncovered, about 10 minutes, or until the sauce has thickened. Remove from heat.

While the sauce is cooking, rinse and trim the scallions. Cut them into 1/4-inch pieces and then set aside.

When the water comes to a boil, add the linguine. Cook according to directions.

About 3 minutes before the linguine is ready, add the scallops to the tomato mixture and cook about 3 minutes, or until they turn white. Add the scallions and stir. Remove from heat.

Drain the linguine and transfer it to the pot with the sauce. Toss until the linguine and sauce are well combined. Distribute the mixture into four bowls and serve immediately.

Mom Tip: Fresh scallops are available at most fish counters. They come in several sizes, the largest being the most expensive. Small scallops, including bay scallops, are about the size of your fingernail and are better suited to this dish. Frozen scallops may not be as succulent as fresh scallops, but they're incredibly convenient. You can often find them in 1-pound bags near the frozen shrimp. Add them to this sauce directly from their frozen state, and they'll only need an extra minute to cook. You can also substitute small shrimp if you can't find scallops. If the shrimp are already cooked, just heat them through in the sauce. If they're not, the cooking time remains the same as with scallops.

Bow Tie Pasta with Hot Sausage Sauce

Serves: 4 ✳

Preparation time: 10 minutes ✳

Cooking time: 11 minutes plus 12 minutes for bow ties
(sauce and pasta overlap cooking time) ✳

Time-saving tip: Use a quicker-cooking pasta such as spaghetti, linguine or fettuccine. ✳

Some pasta dishes leave you feeling hungry. Not this one. This is pasta for when you've just worked a double shift in a coal mine. This is pasta for when you're about to compete in the Iditarod. Cook Bow Tie Pasta with Hot Sausage Sauce and you won't have to prepare a side dish.

1 tablespoon olive oil

1/2 pound bulk sausage meat or 4 hot Italian sausages (about 1/2 pound total)

2 teaspoons bottled crushed garlic

1/4 teaspoon red pepper flakes

2 cups meatless spaghetti sauce

1/2 cup water

16 ounces bow tie (farfalle) pasta

1/2 cup heavy cream

Grated Parmesan cheese

Fill a large pot with water, cover and begin heating over high heat.

While the water is heating, put the olive oil into a large frying pan or wok and begin heating over medium-high heat. Add the sausage and then break it into small pieces with a wooden spoon. If you are using Italian sausages, cut the casings off and discard them and then break the sausages into small pieces. Add the garlic and red pepper flakes and cook about 5 minutes, stirring occasionally, or until the sausage meat browns. Add the spaghetti sauce and water and stir briefly. Turn down to low heat, cover and cook for 5 minutes. Remove from heat and then set aside.

When the water comes to a boil, add the pasta and cook according to directions. Just before the bow ties are done, add the cream to the sauce, bring to a boil and cook for 1 minute. Remove from heat.

When the bow ties are cooked, drain them and distribute into four bowls. Top with the sausage sauce and serve immediately with Parmesan cheese sprinkled over top.

Fusilli with Asparagus and Artichoke Hearts

Serves: 4

Preparation time: 10 minutes ✳

Cooking time: 6 minutes for sauce plus 12 minutes for fusilli
(sauce and fusilli overlap cooking time) ✳

Time-saving tip: Use a mini food processor to chop the parsley. ✳

There are so many different kinds of pasta. Does this dish absolutely require that you use fusilli and not farfalle? I don't think so. So, go ahead and be different. The recipe doesn't rule your world. And while you're at it, go ahead and use 2 1/2 teaspoons of garlic instead of 2. See how good that feels? Or you could just follow the recipe and not worry about it. I can assure you it tastes good that way.

1 large onion

1 pound asparagus

1/4 pound thin-sliced salami or prosciutto

1 14-ounce can artichoke hearts

1/2 cup fresh parsley

1/4 cup olive oil

2 teaspoons bottled crushed garlic

1/4 teaspoon red pepper flakes

1/4 teaspoon black pepper

3 tablespoons bottled lemon juice

8 ounces fusilli

Grated Parmesan cheese

Fill a large pot with water, cover and begin heating over high heat.

While the water is heating, peel the onion and cut it into 1/2-inch pieces. Rinse and trim the asparagus and cut it into 1-inch pieces. Cut the salami or prosciutto into 1/4-inch strips. Drain the artichokes and cut them into quarters. Rinse the parsley. Cut off and discard the stems and cut the leafy parts into 1/2-inch pieces and then set aside.

Put the olive oil into a large frying pan or wok and begin heating over medium-high heat. Add the onion, asparagus, garlic, red pepper flakes and black pepper and cook about 5 minutes, stirring occasionally, or until the vegetables begin to soften. Add the salami or prosciutto and artichoke hearts and cook for 1 minute. Add the lemon juice and parsley, cover and remove from heat.

When the water comes to a boil, add the fusilli and cook according to directions. Drain the fusilli and distribute into four bowls. Top with the sauce and serve immediately with Parmesan cheese sprinkled over top.

Mom Tip: To vary the flavor or make the sauce go further, add 1 sliced red pepper, 1/2 pound presliced mushrooms or 1 cup sliced bok choy when you add the onion.

Linguine with White Clam Sauce

Serves: 4 ✳

Preparation time: 5 minutes ✳

Cooking time: 5 minutes for sauce plus 8 minutes for linguine
(sauce and linguine overlap cooking time) ✳

Time-saving tip: Use fresh linguine, which cooks in 3 minutes. Because fresh noodles weigh more, you will need 1 1/2 pounds to serve 4 people. ✳

My dad is incapable of cooking anything without clams in it. He decided to make clams his specialty and never progressed beyond them. If my mom was out of town and there was a clam shortage, she'd return to find him surviving on crumbs that had fallen under the dinner table. Luckily, clams are plentiful. Linguine with White Clam Sauce is an excellent pasta dish and it's so easy, my dad can make it.

1 1/2 cups fresh parsley

2 tablespoons olive oil

2 tablespoons bottled crushed garlic

1 8-ounce bottle clam juice

2 6 1/2-ounce cans minced or chopped clams

1/4 teaspoon black pepper

16 ounces linguine

Fill a large pot with water, cover and begin heating over high heat.

While the water is heating, rinse the parsley. Cut off and discard the stems and cut the leafy parts into 1/2-inch pieces and then set aside.

Put the olive oil into a frying pan and begin heating over medium-high heat. Add the garlic and cook about 30 seconds, or until it begins to sizzle. Add the bottled clam juice and any juice drained from the clams. Cook about 5 minutes so that the juice cooks down a little and the flavor intensifies. Add the clams, parsley and black pepper and remove from heat and then set aside.

When the water comes to a boil, add the linguine and cook according to directions.

Drain the linguine and transfer to four plates. Top with the clam sauce and serve immediately.

Pasta Carbonara

Serves: 4 ✳

Preparation time: 5 minutes ✳

Cooking time: 15 minutes for sauce plus 8–12 minutes for pasta
(sauce and pasta overlap cooking time) ✳

Time-saving tip: Use precooked bacon. ✳

It's unusual to have ham, eggs, peas and red wine in a pasta sauce. No tomatoes, no meatballs, no clams. It's a different taste entirely. It seems like you should need a permit to vary so dramatically from standard noodle preparation. But maybe one day Pasta Carbonara will be the norm. Give it a try.

1/4 pound prosciutto or 12-ounce package regular bacon or turkey bacon

1 tablespoon olive oil (optional)

1/4 cup red wine

1 cup frozen peas

16 ounces pasta (spaghetti, fusilli, penne)

3 large eggs

1 teaspoon bottled crushed garlic

1/2 teaspoon black pepper

1/4 cup grated Parmesan cheese

Fill a large pot with water, cover and begin heating over high heat.

While the water is heating, cut the prosciutto or bacon into 1-inch pieces and put into a heavy frying pan. If using prosciutto, add the olive oil so the prosciutto doesn't burn. Cook over medium-high heat about 10 minutes, or until the pieces are crisp.

Leave the prosciutto or bacon in the pan but drain and discard all but 1 tablespoon fat. Add the wine and stir, scraping up any bits that have stuck to the pan. Add the unthawed peas, turn down to medium-low heat and cook about 4 minutes, or until they are warmed through.

When the water comes to a boil, add the pasta and cook according to directions.

While the pasta is cooking, beat the eggs in a small bowl for a few seconds. Add the garlic and black pepper, stir and then set aside.

Drain the pasta and immediately return it to the pot. Pour the egg mixture over the hot pasta and let sit for 1 minute. Toss the pasta well. The heat of the pasta will cook the eggs, which will lightly coat the pasta. Add the bacon-wine-pea mixture and Parmesan cheese, toss again and serve immediately.

Penne with Indian-Style Cauliflower Sauce

Serves: 4 ✳

Preparation time: 10 minutes ✳

Cooking time: 8 minutes for sauce plus 12 minutes
for penne (sauce and penne overlap cooking time) ✳

Time-saving tip: Use a 16-ounce package frozen cauliflower
or precut cauliflower from the grocery store's salad bar. ✳

Genuine Indian food doesn't use pasta. Genuine Italian food doesn't sprinkle on cumin and turmeric. Penne with Indian-Style Cauliflower Sauce is a true melting pot recipe. It takes tastes from two continents and makes them work really well together.

1 small or 1/2 large cauliflower

1 medium onion

1 16-ounce can tomato sauce

1 teaspoon ground coriander

1/2 teaspoon ground cumin

1/2 teaspoon ground turmeric

1/2 teaspoon salt

1/4 teaspoon black pepper

1/8 teaspoon ground cloves

Dash cayenne pepper

1/4 cup sour cream

8 ounces penne

Fill a large pot with water, cover and begin heating over high heat.

While the water is heating, trim and discard the leaves and core from the cauliflower. Cut the rest into bite-size pieces and then set aside.

Peel the onion and cut it into quarters. Put the onion and tomato sauce into the bowl of a food processor or blender and process until smooth.

Pour the onion mixture into a large pot. Add the cauliflower, coriander, cumin, turmeric, salt, black pepper, cloves and cayenne pepper and begin cooking over medium-high heat. Cook about 8 minutes, stirring occasionally, or until the cauliflower is soft enough to be pierced with a sharp knife. Add the sour cream and stir. Remove from heat and cover until needed.

When the water comes to a boil, add the penne and cook according to directions. Drain it and distribute into four bowls. Top with the cauliflower sauce and serve immediately.

Spaghetti with Olives and Capers

Serves: 4

Preparation time: 5 minutes

Cooking time: 15 minutes for sauce plus 6 minutes for spaghetti (sauce and spaghetti overlap cooking time)

Time-saving tip: Use prechopped olives.

Both olives and capers are native to the Mediterranean area. The ancient Romans used to snack on them when they weren't building aqueducts and dodging thunderbolts from Mount Olympus. They weren't combined with spaghetti until modern times, but it's nice to enjoy a meal with classic Mediterranean taste. The toga is optional.

20 kalamata olives (see Mom Tip 1)

2 tablespoons capers

1 28-ounce can ready-cut tomatoes

2 tablespoons bottled crushed garlic

1 tablespoon olive oil

1/4 teaspoon black pepper

1/4 teaspoon cayenne pepper

1/2 cup fresh basil

16 ounces spaghetti rigati (see Mom Tip 2)

Fill a large pot with water, cover and begin heating over high heat.

While the water is heating, cut the olives in half and discard any pits. Rinse the capers. Put the olives, capers, tomatoes and their juice, garlic, olive oil, black pepper and cayenne pepper into a medium pot and bring the mixture to a boil over high heat. Turn down to medium heat and cook about 15 minutes, or until the mixture thickens and is no longer watery. Remove from heat.

Rinse the basil, cut it into thin strips and then add to the tomato mixture.

When the water comes to a boil, add the spaghetti rigati and cook according to directions.

Drain the spaghetti rigati and transfer to four plates. Top with the olive and caper sauce and serve immediately.

Mom Tip 1: Kalamata olives are black and come from Greece. They are available in cans or at some deli counters. They have a stronger, saltier flavor than American-style olives.

Mom Tip 2: Spaghetti rigati, a new pasta with ridges introduced by Barilla, was designed to capture more sauce. But the ridges cut spaghetti's cooking time by nearly half. If you can't find it, use regular spaghetti or angel hair (vermicelli) pasta.

Spaghetti with Spicy Zucchini Sauce

Serves: 4

Preparation time: 15 minutes

Cooking time: 10 minutes for sauce plus 8 minutes for spaghetti
(sauce and spaghetti overlap cooking time)

Time-saving tip: Use fresh noodles, which cook in 2–3 minutes. Because fresh noodles weigh more, you will need 1 1/2 pounds to serve 4 people.

My wife and I got into a rut a few years ago with spaghetti. We would cook up some noodles and just add a jar of store-bought sauce. It was quick, as easy as can be, and it almost felt like cooking. But, wow, was it boring. Here's a spaghetti recipe that's almost as quick and easy, but infinitely more interesting.

4 large zucchini

1 large onion

1/2 cup fresh parsley

2 tablespoons olive oil

1/2 teaspoon red pepper flakes

1/2 teaspoon salt

1/4 teaspoon black pepper

2 teaspoons bottled crushed garlic

16 ounces spaghetti

Grated Parmesan cheese

Fill a large pot with water, cover and begin heating over high heat.

While the water is heating, rinse and trim the ends of the zucchini and then cut it into 2-inch-long, 1/4-inch-wide strips. Peel the onion and cut it into 1/4-inch pieces. Rinse the parsley. Cut off and discard the stems and cut the leafy parts into 1/2-inch pieces and then set aside.

Put the olive oil into a wok or large frying pan and begin heating over medium-high heat. Add the red pepper flakes, salt and black pepper and cook about 30 seconds, or until the spices have dissolved. Add the garlic and stir for a few seconds. Add the onion and cook, stirring occasionally, about 5 minutes, or until it has begun to soften. Add the zucchini and cook, stirring occasionally, about 5 minutes, or until it has softened. Remove from heat, stir in the parsley and cover until needed.

When the water comes to a boil, add the spaghetti and cook according to directions.

Drain the spaghetti and distribute into four bowls. Top with the zucchini sauce and serve immediately with Parmesan cheese sprinkled over top.

Tortellini with Spinach and Goat Cheese

Serves: 4–6 ✳

Preparation time: 10 minutes ✳

Cooking time: 12–15 minutes (despite what package might say) ✳

Time-saving tip: Use fresh tortellini, which cooks faster. Because fresh tortellini weighs more, you will need 1 1/2 pounds to serve 4 people. ✳

With tortellini, as with ravioli, you're halfway done cooking before you start (unless you want to spend all night stuffing your own pasta). So, all that's left to add is a little sauce. This sauce has a few ingredients (pine nuts, goat cheese) that I might not have thought to include in my younger, blander years, but these days I'm more adventurous. Just because I want to eat soon doesn't mean I always want to eat the same old thing.

1 16-ounce package dried tortellini

1 6-ounce bag (about 8 cups) fresh prewashed spinach

1/2 cup pine nuts

1/2 cup (4 ounces) goat cheese (see Mom Tip)

1/4 cup olive oil

2 tablespoons bottled lemon juice

1/2 teaspoon salt

1/4 teaspoon black pepper

Fill a large pot with water, cover and begin heating over high heat.

While the water is heating, put 2 cups loosely packed spinach, goat cheese, pine nuts, oil, lemon juice, salt and black pepper into the bowl of a food processor or blender. Process until smooth and then set aside.

When the water boils, add the tortellini and cook about 12–15 minutes, no matter what the directions say. Overcooked tortellini is mushy. Tortellini should be firm. About 1 minute before tortellini is done, add the remaining spinach to the pot.

Drain the tortellini and spinach and return to the pot. Add the processed spinach mixture and stir until well combined. The heat of the tortellini will cause the cheese in the spinach mixture to melt. Serve immediately, or set aside until ready to eat, and then reheat briefly.

> **Mom Tip:** If goat cheese is not available, use feta or blue cheese.

Rice, Beans, Grains & Tofu

Rice, beans, grains, and tofu may sound like a lost '60s' folk group, or at least the foods that would be eaten by lost '60s' folk groups. But there are choices here that would appeal to people who don't even own sandals. Indian Fried Rice, Southwest-Style Felafel and North African Vegetable Couscous, among others, give an international flavor to any meal.

Indian Fried Rice

Risotto

Red Beans and Rice

Spicy Garbanzo Beans

French Country-Style Lentils with Bacon

North African Vegetable Couscous

Southwest-Style Felafel

Kung Pao Tofu

Indian Fried Rice

Serves: 4

Preparation time: 20 minutes (including cooking the rice) ✳

Cooking time: 13 minutes (preparation and cooking times overlap) ✳

Time-saving tip: Use leftover rice. ✳

My mom discovered this recipe (which is also known as Kedgeree) in England, where we lived for many years. I remember her dragging my sister and me to the Tachbrook Street Market every Saturday morning, where the bellicose fishmonger would poke the eye of some poor smoked fish and snarl as he wrapped it up. I used to be scared to death of that man. In America, smoked fish is easily available, without the emotional distress, in cans near the tuna. Kippers add a lot of flavor to this fried rice recipe, but can easily be left out for vegetarians.

1 1/2 cups uncooked white rice or 3 cups leftover cooked white or brown rice

2 large eggs

1 large onion

2 medium carrots (optional)

1/2 cup fresh cilantro (optional)

3 tablespoons olive or corn oil

2 teaspoons curry powder

Dash cayenne pepper

2 3-ounce cans kipper fillets or smoked kipper snacks (see Mom Tip)

1/2 teaspoon salt

1/4 teaspoon black pepper

Cold leftover rice is better for this dish, but if it is unavailable, cook the rice first according to package directions (see page 241).

While the rice is cooking, scramble the eggs and let cool. Cut the cooked eggs small pieces and then set aside.

Peel the onion and cut it into 1/2-inch pieces. Peel or scrub the carrots, if using, and slice them as thinly as possible. Rinse and pat dry the cilantro, if using. Cut off and discard the stems and cut the leafy parts into 1/2-inch pieces and then set aside.

Begin heating the oil in a large frying pan or wok over medium-high heat. Add the onion and carrots, if using, and cook about 5 minutes, stirring occasionally, or until the vegetables begin to soften. Add the curry powder and cayenne pepper and stir.

Add the rice to the onion mixture and cook about 3 minutes, stirring occasionally, or until hot and beginning to brown. Add the kippers and their liquid and continue stirring. Break the kippers into 1/2-inch pieces with the spatula. Add the egg, cilantro, if using, salt and black pepper and stir until hot. Serve immediately or set aside until ready to eat, and then reheat briefly.

Mom Tip: Smoked fish, including haddock, mackerel and trout, is available in vacuum-sealed packages in refrigerated cases near the fish counter at some grocery stores. You can add more than 6 ounces of fish to this dish, if you like.

Risotto

Serves: 4 ✳

Preparation time: 5 minutes ✳

Cooking time: 20 minutes ✳

Time-saving tip: Use frozen chopped onions. ✳

There are faster ways to cook rice. You can get some bland white lumps in just a few minutes, if that's what you're after. But there are ways to make rice that aren't just ways to soak up gravy. At the top of the list is Risotto. It requires Arborio rice, which can be slightly more difficult to locate. And you have to stand there stirring for 20 minutes in order to get it right. But what you get is the polar opposite of "plain" rice.

1 small onion

5 cups chicken broth OR 5 chicken bouillon cubes, 5 teaspoons chicken bouillon granules or 5 teaspoons chicken base plus 5 cups water (see Mom Tip 1)

5 tablespoons butter, divided

2 cups Italian Arborio rice (see Mom Tip 2)

1 cup dry white wine

1/2 cup grated Parmesan cheese

1 tablespoon chopped fresh basil or parsley

1/2 teaspoon salt

1/4 teaspoon black pepper

Peel the onion and cut it into 1/2-inch pieces.

Heat the chicken broth in a medium saucepan and keep warm over low heat.

Melt 4 tablespoons of the butter in a large, heavy-bottomed saucepan. When the butter foams, add the onion. Cook over medium heat about 5 minutes, or until the onion softens.

Add the rice and cook for 2 minutes, or just enough to coat the rice with the butter. Stir in the wine. Cook about 1 minute, stirring constantly, or until the wine has evaporated. Add a few ladles of broth, just enough to cover the rice. Cook over medium heat, stirring constantly, until the broth has been absorbed.

Continue cooking and stirring the rice in this manner, adding broth a bit at a time, until the rice is done. This will take 15–20 minutes. The rice should be tender but still firm to the bite and have a creamy, moist consistency. Add the remaining tablespoon butter, Parmesan cheese, basil or parsley, salt and black pepper and stir until the butter has melted. Serve immediately.

Mom Tip 1: Fernanda Capraro, who owns Villa Romano Trattoria in Laguna Beach, gave me this recipe. She says it is almost impossible to calculate the exact amount of liquid needed to cook Risotto. There are a lot of variables, so it is always better to have some extra broth on hand. If you run out of broth, substitute boiling water.

Mom Tip 2: Arborio is a medium-grain rice that gives off a lot of starch, which makes the Risotto creamy and slightly sticky. It's a specialty rice that is stocked either with regular rice or in the gourmet section. Its main use is for Risotto.

Mom Tip 3: To make Risotto more substantial, add 1 to 2 cups of one of the following ingredients when you add the remaining butter at the end of cooking: small, cooked shrimp; cooked sliced mushrooms; cooked asparagus cut into 1-inch pieces; cooked, quartered artichoke hearts.

Red Beans and Rice

{
Serves: 4 ✳

Preparation time: 20 minutes (including cooking the rice) ✳

Cooking time: 15 minutes (almost completely overlaps with preparation time) ✳

Time-saving tip: Use leftover rice. ✳

There's very little that a 33-year-old dad and an 18-month-old baby can agree on at dinnertime. He usually disdains my grown-up menu of carefully prepared entrees and side dishes, and I'm certainly not going to try his jars of pureed peas. But here's one recipe we both like. It's a hearty mixture of favorites that he and I can eat together. I still have slightly better table manners.

1 1/2 cups uncooked white rice

1 medium onion

1/4 pound prosciutto

2 tablespoons olive or corn oil

2 teaspoons bottled crushed garlic

1 28-ounce can red beans (see Mom Tip 1)

1 15-ounce can ready-cut tomatoes

1 teaspoon thyme

1/4 teaspoon hot pepper sauce

1/2 cup fresh parsley

Cook the rice first according to package directions (see page 241).

While the rice is cooking, peel the onion and cut it into 1/2-inch pieces. Cut the prosciutto into 1/4-inch strips.

Put the oil into a large pot and begin heating over medium-high heat. Add the onion, prosciutto and garlic and cook about 5 minutes, stirring occasionally, or until the onion begins to soften.

Drain the beans and rinse them under cold running water. Add them to the onion mixture. Then add the tomatoes and their juice, thyme and hot pepper sauce and mix well. Turn down to medium heat and cook, uncovered, for 10 minutes. Stir occasionally and mash some of the beans to thicken the mixture.

Meanwhile, rinse the parsley. Cut off and discard the stems and cut the leafy parts into 1/2-inch pieces. Just before serving, add the rice to the bean mixture and mix well. Sprinkle with parsley. Serve immediately or set aside until ready to eat, and then reheat briefly.

Mom Tip 1: Black beans are a good substitute.

Mom Tip 2: One cup leftover cooked chicken, ham, pork or sausage makes this dish even more substantial.

Spicy Garbanzo Beans

Serves: 4 *

Preparation time: 10 minutes *

Cooking time: 10 minutes *

Time-saving tip: Use bottled masala simmer sauce (see Mom Tip 2 with Chicken Tikka, page 147) instead of making the sauce. *

These aren't garbanzo beans for beginners. These garbanzo beans are for those people who've had it with regular blah garbanzo beans. Spicy Garbanzo Beans will make you sit up straight in your chair.

1 large onion

2 tablespoons olive or corn oil

1 teaspoon bottled crushed garlic

1 teaspoon ground ginger

1 teaspoon paprika

1/2 teaspoon ground cumin

1/2 teaspoon ground turmeric

1/2 teaspoon salt

1/8 teaspoon cayenne pepper

1 8-ounce can tomato sauce

1 tablespoon lemon juice

2 15-ounce cans garbanzo beans

1/4 cup sour cream

Handful fresh cilantro (optional)

Peel the onion and cut it into 1/4-inch slices.

Put the oil into a large frying pan or wok and begin heating over medium-high heat. Add the onion and cook about 5 minutes, stirring occasionally, or until it begins to soften.

Add the garlic, ginger, paprika, cumin, turmeric, salt and cayenne pepper and mix well. Cook for 30 seconds. Add the tomato sauce and lemon juice and bring to a boil. Turn down to low heat, cover and cook for 5 minutes.

Drain the garbanzo beans, rinse them under cold running water and then add them to the sauce. Add the sour cream, mix well and bring the mixture back to a boil over medium-high heat. Turn down to low heat, cover and cook 5 minutes more.

If you are using fresh cilantro, rinse and pat it dry. Cut off and discard the stems and then cut the leafy parts into 1/2-inch pieces.

Remove the bean mixture from the heat, sprinkle with cilantro, if using, and serve immediately. Or set aside until ready to eat, and then reheat briefly.

French Country-Style Lentils with Bacon

Serves: 4 ✳

Preparation time: 10 minutes ✳

Cooking time: 20 minutes (overlaps with preparation time) ✳

Time-saving tip: Cook the bacon in strips. ✳

Bacon isn't the healthiest food on the planet. There's no sense dancing around it. But, boy does it taste good as an occasional treat. Luckily, the healthiest food is . . . lentils! Like an angel on one shoulder and a devil on the other, lentils and bacon can now battle for your mortal taste buds. And the winner is . . . you.

2 cups dried brown lentils

2 14-ounce cans beef broth OR 3 beef bouillon cubes, 3 teaspoons beef bouillon granules or 3 teaspoons beef base plus 3 1/2 cups water

5 ounces frozen whole baby onions OR 2 large peeled onions, cut into quarters

1 8- to 10-ounce package peeled baby carrots

12 slices bacon

2 teaspoons bottled crushed garlic

1/2 teaspoon black pepper

Put the lentils, beef broth, onions and carrots into a large pot and bring to a boil over high heat. Turn down to low heat, cover and cook about 20 minutes, or until the lentils are soft enough to chew. Check the lentils after 15 minutes to make sure the liquid hasn't boiled away. Add 1/4 cup or more boiling water if necessary. However, there should be almost no liquid left at the end of cooking. If there is, remove the lid, turn up to high heat and stir until the excess water evaporates.

While the lentils are cooking, cut the bacon slices into 1-inch pieces and cook in a small, heavy-bottomed pot over medium-high heat about 10 minutes, or until the pieces are crisp. Spoon most of the bacon fat away, leaving about 1 tablespoon in the bottom of the pot. Add the garlic and black pepper and stir for a few seconds, or until the garlic begins to sizzle. Remove from heat and then set aside until needed.

When the lentil mixture is ready, pour the bacon mixture over it and mix well. Serve immediately, or cover and serve when needed.

North African Vegetable Couscous

Serves: 4 ✳

Preparation time: 15 minutes ✳

Cooking time: 10 minutes ✳

Time-saving tip: Use frozen chopped onions and peeled baby carrots. ✳

Couscous. It's more than just fun to say. It's an easy-to-prepare dish-in-a-box that takes on the flavor of what it's cooked with, in this case vegetable broth. It may look and act like rice, but it's actually made out of wheat, like pasta. It's easy to vary the vegetables that you mix in, but we like this combination.

1 medium onion

2 medium carrots

1 large or 2 small zucchini

3 tablespoons olive or corn oil

1 teaspoon bottled crushed garlic

1 teaspoon salt

1/2 teaspoon black pepper

1 15-ounce can garbanzo beans

1 14-ounce can vegetable broth OR 2 vegetable bouillon cubes, 2 teaspoons vegetable bouillon granules or 2 teaspoons vegetable base plus 2 cups water

1 cup uncooked couscous

1/4 teaspoon harissa plus more if desired (see Mom Tip)

Peel the onion and cut it into 1-inch pieces. Peel the carrots and cut them into 1/2-inch rounds. Rinse the zucchini, trim and discard the ends and then cut it into 1/2-inch slices.

Put the oil into a large frying pan and begin heating over medium-high heat. Add the onion and carrots and cook about 5 minutes, stirring occasionally, or until the vegetables have begun to soften. Add the zucchini, garlic, salt and black pepper and cook another 2 minutes. Remove from heat.

Drain the garbanzo beans and rinse them under cold running water. Add them to the vegetable mixture, mix well, cover and then set aside.

Heat the vegetable broth in a small pot. Put the couscous into a large serving bowl. When the broth is hot, pour 1 cup of it over the couscous, stir the mixture briefly and cover the bowl with plastic wrap. Let stand at least 5 minutes. Add 1/4 teaspoon harissa to the remaining broth and transfer the broth to a gravy boat or small pitcher.

Just before serving, add the vegetables to the couscous and mix well. Offer the spicy broth as gravy.

Mom Tip: Harissa is a North African hot chile paste made of chiles, garlic and olive oil and is often sold in bottles in gourmet food shops. Hot pepper sauce can be used as a substitute.

Southwest-Style Felafel

Serves: 3–4 ✳

Preparation time: 12 minutes ✳

Cooking time: 12 minutes ✳

Time-saving tip: Use two frying pans so you can cook more at once.

I'm always a little suspicious when I like a food but can't name a single ingredient. Perhaps it's because I saw *Soylent Green* at a formative age. Felafel fell into that mystery category. I was relieved to discover that this North African dish is made of garbanzo beans and other items that I commonly keep in the kitchen. It's also an easy recipe to customize, as we have done by adding corn and red pepper for that Southwestern flavor.

1 15-ounce can garbanzo beans

1 medium red bell pepper

1/2 cup fresh cilantro or 1 teaspoon ground coriander

2 teaspoons bottled ginger or 1 teaspoon ground ginger

1 teaspoon dried mint

1 teaspoon salt

1/2 teaspoon black pepper

1/4 teaspoon cayenne pepper

1/3 cup seasoned bread crumbs

1 8-ounce can whole-kernel corn

2 tablespoons olive or corn oil plus more if needed

Drain the garbanzo beans and rinse them under cold running water. Rinse the bell pepper, cut it in half, remove and discard the stem and seeds and then cut it into quarters. Rinse and pat dry the cilantro, if using, and then cut off and discard the stems.

Put the garbanzo beans, bell pepper, cilantro or coriander, ginger, mint, salt, black pepper and cayenne pepper into the bowl of a food processor and process about 1 minute, or until the mixture is finely ground. Add the bread crumbs and process another 30 seconds, or until the mixture is well combined. Drain the corn, add to the mixture and pulse a few times to distribute the kernels but not grind them up. If the mixture is too dry to stick together, add 2 tablespoons water and pulse a few times.

Divide the mixture into eighths and shape each into a 4-inch flat patty.

Put 1 tablespoon of the olive oil into a large frying pan and begin heating over medium-high heat. When hot, add as many of the patties as will fit in one layer and cook for 3 minutes per side, or until they begin to brown. Serve immediately or transfer to a plate and keep warm in the oven while cooking the rest of the patties. Add more oil as needed.

Kung Pao Tofu

Serves: 3–4 ✳

Preparation time: 10 minutes ✳

Cooking time: 15 minutes ✳

Time-saving tip: Use frozen red bell pepper slices and frozen snow peas. ✳

When I think Kung Pao, I don't necessarily think tofu. Kung Pao Chicken and Kung Pao Beef are staples of any food court junkie's diet. But tofu? How modern! Not everybody likes tofu. My mom loves it, while my dad doesn't. He grew up in a meat-and-potatoes house, and the very idea of tofu would have made my grandpa go to the gun rack. But my wife and I both really like it, so this recipe is perfect for us. The homemade Kung Pao sauce has a lot of ingredients, but it's actually quick to make and is better than anything you can buy.

1 14-ounce package firm tofu (see Mom Tip)

1 medium red bell pepper

1/4 pound snow peas

4 scallions

2 tablespoons peanut or corn oil

1/4 teaspoon red pepper flakes

1 teaspoon bottled crushed garlic

1 teaspoon bottled ginger or 1/2 teaspoon ground ginger

3 tablespoons soy sauce

2 tablespoons sugar

1 teaspoon sesame oil

2 teaspoons water

1 teaspoon cornstarch

1/4 to 1/2 cup dry roasted peanuts

Drain the tofu, wrap it in paper towels to absorb excess moisture and then set aside on a large plate until needed.

Rinse the bell pepper, cut it in half, remove and discard the stem and seeds and then cut it into 1/2-inch pieces. Rinse the snow peas, trim and discard the ends and pull off and discard any fibrous strings along the seams. Rinse and trim the scallions and cut them into 1/2-inch pieces.

Cut the tofu into 1/2-inch cubes and then set aside.

Put the oil into a wok or large frying pan and begin heating over medium-high heat. Add the red pepper flakes and bell pepper and cook about 5 minutes, stirring occasionally, or until the bell pepper begins to soften. Add the garlic, ginger and tofu and cook for 5 minutes, turning occasionally. Add the snow peas, soy sauce, sugar and sesame oil and bring to a boil over high heat. Turn down to medium heat and cook, uncovered, stirring occasionally, for 5 minutes.

Meanwhile, put the water and cornstarch into a small cup and stir until the cornstarch dissolves. When the tofu has finished cooking, add the cornstarch mixture and stir gently about 1 minute, or until the tofu mixture thickens. Sprinkle on the scallions and peanuts, stir and serve immediately. Or set aside until ready to eat, and then reheat briefly. To prevent the peanuts from getting soggy, add them just before serving.

Mom Tip: Be sure to use firm tofu. Soft tofu will fall apart.

Poultry

As much as I loved the movie *Chicken Run* and was rooting for the chickens to escape their fate, the truth is I'm glad chickens aren't that elusive. I love to eat chicken and turkey. That's why we have so many choices in this section. From Moroccan Chicken to Russian Chicken Sticks to Chicken Tikka, we've selected recipes from around the world that satisfy the poultry craving. You can never have too many chicken recipes.

Ground Poultry:

Chicken Chili

Popeye Turkeyburgers

Thai-Style Ground Turkey
in Lettuce Leaves

Turkey Meatballs

Boneless Stir-Fry:

Chicken Arrabbiato

Moroccan Chicken

Stir-Fried Chicken
with Bok Choy

Boneless Pan-Fried:

Chinese Lemon Chicken

Chicken with Orange Sauce

Tarragon Chicken

Baked or Grilled:

Barbecued Chicken Thighs

Chicken Tikka

Russian Chicken Sticks

Simple Baked Chicken Breasts

Chicken Chili

Serves: 4 ✳

Preparation time: 10 minutes ✳

Cooking time: 10 minutes ✳

Time-saving tip: Use frozen chopped onions. ✳

Chili purists might scoff at the idea of using chicken instead of beef. But I make it a point not to mind other people scoffing. The truth is, Chicken Chili is a great, hearty one-dish meal that's just a little different from what you're used to. No scoffing allowed.

1 large onion

1 15-ounce can black beans

1 pound ground chicken or turkey

1/2 cup beer or chicken broth

1/2 cup ketchup

1 tablespoon ground chili powder

1 teaspoon bottled crushed garlic

1/2 teaspoon salt

1/4 teaspoon black pepper

1/4 teaspoon hot pepper sauce plus more if needed

Peel the onion and cut it into 1/2-inch pieces and then set aside. Drain the beans and rinse them under cold running water and then set aside.

Without adding oil, brown the chicken or turkey in a medium-size pot over medium heat, stirring frequently to break the meat into small clumps. After the meat has browned, drain off and discard the fat.

Add the onion, beans, beer or chicken broth, ketchup, chili powder, garlic, salt, black pepper and hot pepper sauce and bring to a boil over high heat. Then turn down to low heat and cook, covered, for 10 minutes. Taste to see if the chili is spicy enough. If not, add a few more drops hot pepper sauce. Serve immediately, or set aside until ready to eat, and then reheat briefly.

Mom Tip: Chicken Chili makes a good filling for tortillas. Sprinkle grated cheddar or Monterey Jack cheese over the filling, if desired.

Popeye Turkeyburgers

Serves: 4 ✳

Preparation time: 15 minutes ✳

Cooking time: 8–10 minutes ✳

Time-saving tip: Make mini-patties, which will cook faster. ✳

In order to get my kids to eat veggies, I have to tell them they're going to get stronger, faster and taller as a result. So they'll take one bite and then try to lift the fridge, or run down the hall to see if they burn up the carpet with their speed. Sometimes they'll scream out, "It's working!" I wish veggies worked that way on me.

Popeye Turkeyburgers, named for the patron saint of spinach, are a great way to get a little green into your diet. The fact that they taste really good means I don't have to do much convincing to get the kids to eat them.

1 10-ounce package frozen spinach

1 pound ground turkey

2 tablespoons crumbled feta or blue cheese

1 teaspoon bottled crushed garlic

1 teaspoon salt

1/4 teaspoon black pepper

1/8 teaspoon cayenne pepper

4 hamburger buns

Preheat the broiler. Make sure the top oven rack is 5–6 inches under the broiling unit. For easy clean-up, line the broiling pan with aluminum foil. Place the broiling pan rack on top of the foil and then set aside. Or heat up your gas grill.

Cook the spinach according to directions, drain and let cool.

Put the spinach, turkey, cheese, garlic, salt, black pepper and cayenne pepper into a large bowl and mix. Shape into four large flat patties.

When the broiler or grill is ready, cook the turkeyburgers about 4–5 minutes per side, or until they are fully cooked. Cut into one to make sure the middle is white, not pink. While the patties are cooking, put the buns onto a baking sheet and set it on a lower shelf in the oven to warm. Serve immediately.

Thai-Style Ground Turkey in Lettuce Leaves

Serves: 4 ✳

Preparation time: 10 minutes ✳

Cooking time: 5 minutes ✳

Time-saving tip: Leave out the sesame seeds. ✳

I'm not generally obsessed with presentation when I cook. I've always figured if the food tasted good it wouldn't matter whether it was served on a silver platter or a paper plate. But this dish does look impressive. The fact that it takes only 15 minutes to prepare only adds to its charms. I'll be serving Thai-Style Ground Turkey in Lettuce Leaves the next time I'm entertaining foreign dignitaries.

8 butter, Boston or Bibb lettuce leaves plus more if desired (see Mom Tip 1)

3 scallions

3 tablespoons lime juice

2 tablespoons fish sauce or soy sauce (see Mom Tip 2)

1 teaspoon sugar

1/4 teaspoon cayenne pepper

1/2 cup fresh cilantro

1/4 cup sesame seeds

1 pound ground turkey

Half-fill a large pot with water and bring to a boil over high heat.

While the water is heating, rinse and pat dry the lettuce leaves and place them on a serving dish.

Rinse and trim the scallions, cut them into 1/2-inch pieces and put them into a large bowl. Add the lime juice, fish or soy sauce, sugar and cayenne pepper and stir and then set aside.

Rinse and pat dry the cilantro. Cut off and discard the stems and cut the leafy parts into 1/2-inch pieces. Put it into a small bowl.

Put the sesame seeds into a small, dry frying pan and begin heating over medium-high heat about 2 minutes, stirring constantly, or until they start to brown. Watch carefully because they burn easily. Remove from heat and transfer to a small cup.

When the water comes to a boil, add the turkey and stir to break it up into small pieces. Turn down to medium heat and cook about 5 minutes, or until the turkey has turned white.

Remove from heat and drain the turkey. Add it to the scallion-lime juice mixture and mix well. Put the bowl and serving spoon on the table, along with the lettuce platter, cilantro and sesame seeds. Diners should spoon some of the mixture into a lettuce leaf, sprinkle with cilantro and sesame seeds and eat immediately.

Mom Tip 1: Butter, Boston and Bibb lettuce are all names for the same lettuce. This type of lettuce has large, thick leaves that can be easily separated from the core and can serve as "bowls." If this type of lettuce is not available, substitute romaine, leaf lettuce or cabbage.

Mom Tip 2: Fish sauce is the Thai version of soy sauce. It is made from anchovies, water and salt. It should be stocked next to the soy sauce at grocery stores and is always available at Asian markets.

Turkey Meatballs

Serves: 4

Preparation time: 10 minutes

Cooking time: 10 minutes

Time-saving tip: The smaller the meatball, the faster it cooks.

My wife Jody is a vegetarian. We've never had a conflict about it, but I do sometimes get antsy if we eat some sort of eggplant dish three nights in a row. Turkey Meatballs are a perfect antidote for eggplant. I like to keep a container of these in the fridge so I can have a tasty carnivorous snack whenever I'm feeling primitive.

1 tablespoon fresh or dried rosemary

1 pound ground turkey

2/3 cup seasoned bread crumbs

1 large egg

2 tablespoons milk

1 tablespoon black pepper (see Mom Tip 1)

1 teaspoon bottled crushed garlic

1 teaspoon salt

1/4 teaspoon red pepper flakes

Place an oven rack in the middle position and preheat the oven to 375 degrees F. For easy clean-up, line a baking sheet with aluminum foil.

Crush the rosemary using a mortar and pestle or break or cut into as small pieces as possible. Put the rosemary, turkey, bread crumbs, egg, milk, black pepper, garlic, salt and red pepper flakes into a large bowl. Shape the mixture into marble-sized meatballs, about 1/2 inch in diameter.

Transfer the meatballs to the baking sheet and bake about 10 minutes, or until the meatballs begin to brown. Remove from oven and serve immediately. Or set aside until ready to eat, and then reheat briefly.

Mom Tip 1: This recipe calls for a lot of black pepper, and the resulting meatballs are quite spicy. If you don't like spicy food, reduce the amount of black pepper to 1 teaspoon or less.

Mom Tip 2: Here's an alternative way to cook these meatballs. Half-fill a large pot with water, cover and begin heating over high heat. When the water comes to a boil, drop the meatballs into the water and cook about 5 minutes, or until they are firm. Remove from water with a slotted spoon and serve immediately. If you want to serve pasta as a side dish, drop the pasta into the boiling water once you've removed the meatballs.

Chicken Arrabbiato

Serves: 4 ✳

Preparation time: 15 minutes ✳

Cooking time: 8–10 minutes ✳

Time-saving tip: Use 1/2 inch thick sliced deli chicken or turkey. ✳

Arrabbiato means "angry" in Italian. I guess I'd be an angry chicken if I knew I was going to be served with tomato and mushroom sauce. What actually makes this chicken "angry" is the spiciness of the red pepper flakes. It's not tremendously spicy, so perhaps it should be called "Slightly Peeved Chicken."

6 dried shiitake mushrooms or 1/2 pound presliced mushrooms (see Mom Tip 1)

4 boneless chicken breast halves (about 1 1/2 pounds)

1 28-ounce can ready-cut tomatoes

1/2 cup red wine

1 teaspoon bottled crushed garlic

1/4 teaspoon red pepper flakes

8 thin slices hard salami

1 4-ounce can sliced black olives

Put the dried shiitake mushrooms, if using, into a bowl of hot water and then set aside for 10 minutes.

Meanwhile, slice the chicken breasts into strips 1/2 inch wide and 2 inches long. Put the chicken strips, tomatoes and their juice, wine, garlic and red pepper flakes into a wok or large frying pan and begin heating over medium-high heat. Cook, uncovered, stirring occasionally, about 5 minutes, or until the chicken is firm and white.

While the chicken is cooking, slice the salami into 1/4-inch-wide strips. Drain the shiitake mushrooms, if using, discarding the liquid, and slice them into 1/4-inch strips. Discard the tough stems. Drain the olives.

Add the salami, mushrooms and olives to the chicken mixture and cook about 2 minutes, or until hot. If you are using fresh mushrooms, cook about 4 minutes, or until the mushrooms begin to soften. Serve immediately or set aside until ready to eat, and then reheat briefly.

Mom Tip 1: Dried shiitake mushrooms are sold in bags in the Asian food aisle of the grocery store. They need to be soaked before use. They're convenient to keep in the cupboard and can always be used in place of fresh mushrooms. They have more flavor and are chewier than regular mushrooms.

Mom Tip 2: If the sauce seems too watery, add 1–2 tablespoons tomato paste to thicken it.

Moroccan Chicken

Serves: 4 ✳

Preparation time: 10 minutes ✳

Cooking time: 7 minutes ✳

Time-saving tip: Use chicken tenders. ✳

There are several unusual flavors in Moroccan Chicken (mint, cinnamon, black bean garlic sauce). For those of us who love chicken and have had it a thousand times, it's nice to find a new, tasty way to eat it. Perhaps it's what the people are eating in the background of *Casablanca,* while Bogart and Bergman are enjoying their close-ups.

6 scallions

4 boneless chicken breast halves (about 1 1/2 pounds)

1/2 cup raisins

1/2 cup pine nuts

1/4 cup bottled lemon juice

1/4 cup olive or corn oil, divided

2 tablespoons chopped fresh mint or 2 teaspoons dried mint

2 teaspoons bottled crushed garlic

2 teaspoons ground cinnamon

1/2 teaspoon red pepper flakes

2 tablespoons Black Bean Garlic Sauce (see Mom Tip)

Rinse and trim the scallions and cut them into 1-inch pieces and then set aside.

Slice the chicken breasts into strips 1/2 inch wide and 2 inches long and put them into a large bowl. Add the raisins, pine nuts, lemon juice, 2 tablespoons oil, mint, garlic, cinnamon and red pepper flakes. Mix well.

Put the remaining 2 tablespoons oil into a wok or large frying pan and begin heating over medium-high heat. Add the chicken mixture and stir-fry for 5–6 minutes, or until the chicken is fully cooked. Test a piece by cutting it in half to make sure the middle is white, not pink. Add the scallion pieces and black bean garlic sauce and mix well. Heat for 1 minute and serve immediately. Or set aside until ready to eat, and then reheat briefly.

Mom Tip: Black Bean Garlic Sauce is available in jars in the Asian food aisle. It is pretty salty, so there's no need to add salt to this dish.

Stir-Fried Chicken with Bok Choy

Serves: 4 ✳

Preparation time: 15 minutes ✳

Cooking time: 10 minutes ✳

Time-saving tip: Use frozen chopped onions. ✳

When I stir-fry, I really feel like I'm cooking. There's no closing the oven door and waiting for some miracle to happen. When you stir-fry, you've got ingredients flying everywhere and you see it all come together before your eyes. It amazes the kids as well, as long as you can keep them away from the wok, which operates on my boys like a tractor beam. This recipe is very satisfying and healthy, which food should be if it possibly can.

4 boneless chicken breast halves (about 1 1/2 pounds)

1 large bok choy (about 1 pound) (see Mom Tip 1)

1 small onion

2 tablespoons peanut or corn oil, divided

1 teaspoon bottled crushed garlic

1/2 teaspoon black pepper

1/4 teaspoon red pepper flakes

2 tablespoons hoisin sauce (see Mom Tip 2)

1 tablespoon soy sauce

1/2 cup water

2 teaspoons cornstarch

1 cup cashew nuts (optional)

Slice the chicken breasts into strips 1/2 inch wide and 2 inches long and then set aside.

Separate the bok choy stalks and rinse them. Trim and discard the bottom inch of the stalks. Cut off the leafy parts and cut them into 1-inch strips. Cut the stalks into 1/4-inch slices. Peel the onion and cut it into 1/2-inch pieces.

Put 1 tablespoon of the oil into a wok or large frying pan and begin heating over medium-high heat. Add the sliced bok choy stalks, onion, garlic, black pepper and red pepper flakes and stir-fry about 3 minutes, or until the vegetables just begin to lose their crispness. Transfer the contents of the wok to a bowl or plate.

Put the remaining tablespoon oil into the wok or frying pan and begin heating over medium-high heat. Add the chicken and stir-fry for 5–6 minutes, or until the chicken is fully cooked. Test a piece by cutting into it to make sure the middle is white, not pink.

Return the cooked vegetables and any liquid to the wok. Add the sliced leafy part of the bok choy, hoisin sauce and soy sauce. Put the water and cornstarch into a cup, stir until the cornstarch dissolves and add it to the wok. Cook, stirring constantly, for 1 minute, or until the liquid at the bottom of the wok thickens. Sprinkle with cashews, if using, and serve immediately. Or set aside until ready to eat, and then reheat briefly. To prevent the cashews from getting soggy, add them just before serving.

Mom Tip 1: Bok choy is a Chinese cabbage. It has white celery-like stalks that end in light or dark green curly leaves. If you can't find any, substitute 4 stalks celery and 2 handfuls fresh spinach.

Mom Tip 2: Hoisin sauce is available in jars in the Asian food aisle.

Chinese Lemon Chicken

Serves: 4 ✳

Preparation time: 12 minutes ✳

Cooking time: 9–13 minutes ✳

Time-saving tip: Cut the chicken breasts into strips 1/2 inch wide and 2 inches long and cook as a stir-fry. ✳

Flattening chicken breasts with a rolling pin is about as violent as I get. Generally I'm mild-mannered, but when a recipe calls for pounding I surge with the hostility of an agitated Tyrannosaurus Rex. Then I'm back to normal. Chinese Lemon Chicken is as good as it sounds. I generally double the recipe because I always want more.

1 lemon

3/4 cup water

1 tablespoon cornstarch

3 tablespoons lemon juice

2 tablespoons brown sugar

1 teaspoon bottled ginger or 1/2 teaspoon ground ginger

1/2 teaspoon sesame oil

1/2 teaspoon salt

4 boneless chicken breast halves (about 1 1/2 pounds)

1 tablespoon peanut or corn oil plus more if needed

Rinse the lemon and cut it into paper-thin slices. Put the water and cornstarch into a small pot and stir until the cornstarch dissolves. Add the lemon juice, brown sugar, ginger, sesame oil and salt and bring to a boil over high heat, stirring constantly about 1 minute, or until the mixture thickens. Add the lemon slices, remove from heat, cover and then set aside.

Cut off and discard any fat attached to the chicken breasts. Put a chicken breast between two pieces of wax paper and pound to 1/2-inch thickness with a rolling pin or the side of a can. Repeat with the other breasts. Or, using a sharp knife, cut 1/2-inch slices lengthwise through each chicken breast, ending up with 2 or 3 thin slices per breast. Don't worry if some of the pieces are smaller than others.

Put 1 tablespoon of the peanut oil into a wok, large frying pan or grill pan with ridges and begin heating over high heat. Cook as many of the chicken breast pieces as will fit into the pan about 2 minutes per side, or until both sides turn white. Test a piece by cutting into it to make sure the middle is white, not pink. Transfer the chicken to a plate and repeat until all the chicken is cooked, adding more oil if necessary.

Transfer the chicken to four plates. Reheat the lemon sauce and pour about half of it over the chicken, making sure at least 2 lemon slices decorate each plate. Put the rest of the sauce into a serving dish and offer it separately. Serve immediately.

Chicken with Orange Sauce

Serves: 4 ✳

Preparation time: 5 minutes ✳

Cooking time: 20 minutes ✳

Time-saving tip: Cut chicken breasts in half so they cook faster. ✳

When I was six years old, I won a spice rack in a school raffle. Most of the spices ran out decades ago, but there are still a few of them left on my mother's counter. One of them is tarragon. In twenty-seven years she's used about a tablespoon of tarragon. She was delighted to get this recipe from Dorothy Samuel. It uses tarragon, along with some other unusual flavors (currants, orange peel) to make a tasty orange sauce.

1/4 cup fresh tarragon or 1 teaspoon dried tarragon

4 boneless chicken breast halves (about 1 1/2 pounds)

2 tablespoons olive or corn oil plus more if needed

2 cups orange juice

1/2 cup dried currants

2 tablespoons freshly grated orange peel or 1 teaspoon dried orange peel (see Mom Tip 1)

1 chicken bouillon cube, 1 teaspoon chicken bouillon granules OR 1 teaspoon chicken base

1/2 teaspoon salt

1/2 teaspoon paprika

1/4 teaspoon black pepper

Rinse the fresh tarragon, if using. Cut off and discard the stems and cut the leafy parts into 1/2-inch pieces and then set aside.

Cut off and discard any fat attached to the chicken breasts.

Put the oil into a wok or large frying pan and begin heating over medium-high heat. Add the chicken breasts and cook for 1 minute per side.

Add the tarragon, orange juice, currants, orange peel, bouillon cube, granules or chicken base, salt, paprika and black pepper and bring to a boil over high heat. Turn down to medium heat, cover and cook about 7 minutes, or until the chicken is firm and white. Test a piece by cutting into it to make sure the middle is white, not pink. Transfer the chicken to a plate and then set aside.

Bring the orange sauce to a boil over high heat and cook about 10 minutes, or until the sauce is reduced by half and has thickened slightly. Return the chicken to the sauce and reheat about 1 minute, or until the chicken is hot. Serve immediately or set aside until ready to eat, and then reheat briefly.

Mom Tip 1: Grating orange and lemon peel used to be a pain until I discovered the Microplane, an easy-to-use stainless steel zester. It looks like a ruler with holes. Just rub it over the surface of an orange or lemon, and the zest flakes right off without damaging your knuckles. It's available at cooking supply stores.

Mom Tip 2: Add sliced zucchini or frozen peas to the orange sauce during the last 5 minutes of cooking for an easy vegetable side dish.

Tarragon Chicken

Serves: 4

Preparation time: 10 minutes

Cooking time: 10–14 minutes

Time-saving tip: Use two frying pans to cook all the chicken at once.

People assume that restaurant food would be impossible to make at home. But this recipe, which comes from chef Fernanda Capraro and is on the menu at her Laguna Beach restaurant Villa Romana Trattoria, proves that it's more than possible. Tarragon Chicken is a dish that you can proudly serve to company at home. How much you charge them is up to you.

1/4 cup fresh tarragon or 1 teaspoon dried tarragon

4 boneless chicken breast halves (about 1 1/2 pounds)

4 tablespoons olive oil plus more if needed

1/2 pound presliced mushrooms

2 tablespoons butter

1/2 cup chicken broth OR 1/2 chicken bouillon cube, 1/2 teaspoon chicken
   bouillon granules or 1/2 teaspoon chicken base plus 1/2 cup water

1/4 cup dry white wine

1/2 teaspoon salt

1/4 teaspoon black pepper

1/4 cup heavy cream

Rinse the fresh tarragon, if using. Cut off and discard the stems and cut the leafy parts into 1/2-inch pieces and then set aside.

Cut off and discard any fat attached to the chicken breasts. Put a chicken breast between two pieces of wax paper and pound to 1/2-inch thickness with a rolling pin or the side of a can. Repeat with the other breasts. Or, using a sharp knife, cut 1/2-inch slices lengthwise through each chicken breast, ending up with 2 or 3 thin slices per breast. Don't worry if some of the pieces are smaller than others.

Heat 2 tablespoons of the olive oil in a wok or large frying pan over medium-high heat. Add the mushrooms and cook about 5 minutes, stirring occasionally, or until they begin to soften. Transfer them to a plate and then set aside.

Add the butter and remaining 2 tablespoons olive oil to the pan. When the butter foams, cook the slices of chicken breast about 2 minutes per side, or until both sides have turned white. Test a piece by cutting into it to make sure the middle is white, not pink. Transfer the chicken to a plate and repeat until all the chicken is cooked, adding more oil if necessary.

Add the chicken broth, white wine, tarragon, salt and black pepper to the pan. Bring the mixture to a boil over high heat. Return the chicken to the pan and continue cooking about 1 minute, or until the chicken is hot. Transfer the chicken to four plates.

Turn down to medium-high heat, add the cream and mushrooms and cook for 1 minute. Spoon the sauce over the chicken and serve immediately.

Barbecued Chicken Thighs

Serves: 4 ✳

Preparation time: 5 minutes ✳

Cooking time: 20 minutes ✳

Time-saving tip: Use boneless chicken breasts and cut the boiling and broiling time in half. ✳

For most of my life I've been a white-meat eater, to the point that I hadn't eaten dark meat for years. It was this recipe that reintroduced me to the other half of the chicken. It tastes really good, especially with barbecue sauce, and is the perfect food for a lazy Sunday afternoon cookout. But you can also cook it indoors on a rainy Monday, and it tastes just as good.

1/2 cup bottled barbecue sauce plus more if needed

1/4 cup water

1 tablespoon olive or corn oil

1/4 teaspoon red pepper flakes

12 boneless, skinless chicken thighs (about 1 1/2 pounds)

Preheat the broiler. Make sure the top oven rack is 5–6 inches under the broiling unit. For easy clean-up, line the broiling pan with aluminum foil. Place the broiling pan rack on top of the foil and then set aside. Or heat up your gas grill.

Put the barbecue sauce, water, oil and red pepper flakes into a medium pot and bring to a boil over high heat. Add the chicken thighs and stir to cover with sauce. Turn down to medium-high heat, cover and cook for 10 minutes.

When the broiler or grill is ready, cook the partly-cooked thighs about 5 minutes per side, or until the thighs begin to brown.

While the thighs are broiling, cook the remaining barbecue sauce for 2 minutes over high heat to kill any bacteria. Cover and then set aside.

Before removing the thighs from the heat, cut into one to make sure it isn't pink in the middle. If it is, cook the thighs another 1–2 minutes and test again. If not, remove from heat and serve immediately with remaining barbecue sauce. Add more bottled barbecue sauce if needed. Or set aside until ready to eat, and then reheat briefly in remaining barbecue sauce.

Chicken Tikka

Serves: 4 ✳

Preparation and waiting time: 17 minutes ✳

Cooking time: 8 minutes ✳

Time-saving tip: Use chicken tenders. ✳

I've come a long way since my mom used to feed me from her purse when our family went to an Indian restaurant. Now she sends me Indian recipes. This one is my favorite. It uses a lot of spices, but they all add up to one great flavor.

1/4 cup plain yogurt

2 tablespoons bottled lemon juice

1 teaspoon crushed bottled garlic

2 teaspoons paprika

1 teaspoon bottled ginger or 1/2 teaspoon ground ginger

1/2 teaspoon ground cumin

1/2 teaspoon garam masala (see Mom Tip 1)

1/4 teaspoon ground turmeric

1/4 teaspoon cayenne pepper

4 boneless chicken breast halves (about 1 1/2 pounds)

Skewers

Put the yogurt, lemon juice, garlic, paprika, ginger, cumin, garam masala, turmeric and cayenne pepper into a large bowl and mix well. Slice the chicken breasts into strips 1/2 inch wide and 2 inches long and add them to the bowl. Stir so that the chicken pieces are covered with the yogurt mixture and then set aside for 10 minutes.

Preheat the broiler. Make sure the top oven rack is in the highest position, just under the broiling unit. For easy clean-up, line the broiling pan with aluminum foil. Place the broiling pan rack on top of the foil and then set aside. Or heat up your gas grill.

When the chicken is done marinating, thread the pieces onto skewers, leaving at least 1/4 inch of space between each piece so the chicken will cook more quickly. Discard the leftover marinade. When the broiler or grill is ready, cook the chicken about 4 minutes per side, or until it is firm and white. Test a piece by cutting it in half to make sure the middle is white, not pink. Serve immediately on the skewers.

Mom Tip 1: Garam masala, which is a blend of many spices including coriander, nutmeg, cinnamon and cardamom, is available in the spice aisle of most grocery stores.

Mom Tip 2: Chicken Tikka Masala is a popular dish in Indian restaurants. Masala simmer sauce is available in bottles or cans in some gourmet food shops and Indian markets. Heat up the sauce in a pot while the chicken is cooking. Then push the pieces off the skewers into the sauce and stir. Serve immediately.

Russian Chicken Sticks

Serves: 4 ✳

Preparation time: 17 minutes ✳

Cooking time: 8 minutes ✳

Time-saving tip: Use chicken tenders. ✳

There should be a Nobel Prize for cooking. If there were they could properly reward the person who invented breaded chicken. People around the world enjoy breaded chicken. It's been a large, happy part of my diet for years. Other potential winners include the person who created seedless grapes and the genius who developed the jelly-insertion device for doughnuts.

Russian cooking frequently involves sour cream, and this recipe follows that path.

1 cup sour cream or plain yogurt

2 tablespoons bottled lemon juice

1 teaspoon bottled crushed garlic

1 teaspoon paprika

1/2 teaspoon salt

1/4 teaspoon hot pepper sauce

4 boneless chicken breast halves (about 1 1/2 pounds)

1 cup seasoned bread crumbs plus more if needed

Place an oven rack in the middle position and preheat the oven to 475 degrees F. Line two baking sheets with aluminum foil for easy cleanup.

Put the sour cream or yogurt, lemon juice, garlic, paprika, salt and hot pepper sauce into a large bowl and mix well.

Slice the chicken breasts into strips 1/2 inch wide and 2 inches long and add them to the bowl. Stir so that the chicken strips are covered with the creamy mixture.

Put half the bread crumbs into a shallow bowl. Roll each chicken strip in the crumbs, coating all surfaces, and place it on a baking sheet. Add more bread crumbs as needed. You will have enough chicken to fill two baking sheets. Discard the leftover marinade.

Bake the chicken for 8 minutes. To make sure it is fully cooked, test a piece by cutting it in half. The middle should be white, not pink. Serve immediately or set aside until ready to eat, and then reheat briefly.

Simple Baked Chicken Breasts

Serves: 4 ✳

Preparation time: 10 minutes ✳

Cooking time: 15 minutes ✳

Time-saving tip: Cut chicken breasts in half so they cook faster. ✳

I love boneless chicken breasts. They make cooking so easy. Why don't they sell boneless cow breasts and boneless pig breasts? I'll have to ask the butcher next time I see him. Anyway, here's an idea for a simple, reliable chicken dish that tastes like it was harder to make.

4 boneless chicken breast halves (about 1 1/2 pounds)

1 lemon

2 tablespoons olive or corn oil

1 teaspoon bottled crushed garlic

1/2 teaspoon salt

1/4 teaspoon black pepper

Place an oven rack in the middle position and preheat the oven to 450 degrees F. For easy clean-up, line a large ovenproof casserole dish or the broiling pan with aluminum foil.

Cut off and discard any fat attached to the chicken breasts. Rinse the lemon and cut it into 1/8-inch slices. Put the oil, garlic, salt and black pepper into a cup and mix well.

Put the chicken breasts in a single layer in the casserole dish or broiling pan and spoon the oil mixture on top. Lay lemon slices on the breasts and bake about 15 minutes, or until the chicken is firm and white. Test a piece by cutting into it to make sure the middle is white, not pink. Large pieces may need to bake another 5 minutes. Serve immediately with the lemon slices in place. Or let cool and serve at room temperature or cold.

Mom Tip: Instead of using lemon slices as the topping, use sliced tomatoes or a few tablespoons salsa.

Meat

Big meat dishes take a long time to cook. You can't roast a turkey or make a pot roast in 25 minutes or less. But that's no reason to become a vegetarian. There are plenty of high-speed dishes, like Quick-Fried Pork Chops and Spicy Skirt Steak, for the impatient meat-lover.

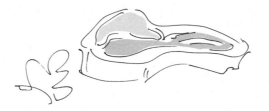

Ground Meat:

Greek Lambburgers

Hamburger Stroganoff

Indian-Style Lamb Kebabs

Steve's Picadillo

Boneless Stir-Fry:

Sausages, Onions and Peppers

Short-Cut Beef Bourguignon

Sweet and Sour Pork with
Broccoli

Skillet-Grilled:

Chinese-Style Pork Medallions

Quick-Fried Pork Chops

Spicy Skirt Steak

Easy Veal Chops

Baked, Roasted or Grilled:

Beef Teriyaki

Grilled Steak Slices

Lamb Souvlakia

Roast Beef in 20 Minutes

Roast Pork Tenderloin

Untraditional Veal Parmesan

Greek Lambburgers

Serves: 4 ✳

Preparation time: 10 minutes ✳

Cooking time: 8 minutes ✳

Time-saving tip: Make mini-patties, which will cook faster. ✳

A lot has happened to hamburgers since their innocent early days. They've become turkey-burgers, mushroom burgers, and tofu burgers. I've had them all, with varying degrees of satisfaction. I have been trained by advertising to believe that burgers will put a smile on my face and bring my family closer together, so I was happy to try them. But I'd never had lambburgers. They were a very pleasant surprise. They have their own taste, and not that of a burger-wannabe.

6 kalamata olives (see Mom Tip)

1 pound ground lamb

1 tablespoon Dijon mustard

2 teaspoons bottled crushed garlic

2 teaspoons dried oregano

1/2 teaspoon salt

1/4 teaspoon black pepper

4 hamburger buns

Preheat the broiler. Make sure the top oven rack is 5–6 inches under the broiling unit. For easy clean-up, line the broiling pan with aluminum foil. Place the broiling pan rack on top of the foil and then set aside. Or heat up your gas grill.

Cut each olive into 6 or 8 pieces and discard any pits.

Put the olive pieces, lamb, mustard, garlic, oregano, salt and black pepper into a large bowl and mix well. Shape into four large flat patties.

When the broiler or grill is ready, cook the lambburgers about 3–4 minutes per side, or until they begin to brown. They can be a little pink in the middle. While the patties are cooking, put the buns onto a baking sheet and set on a lower shelf in the oven to warm. Serve immediately.

Mom Tip: *Kalamata olives are black and come from Greece. They are available in cans or at some deli counters. They have a stronger, saltier flavor than American-style olives.*

Hamburger Stroganoff

Serves: 4 ✳

Preparation Time: 5 minutes ✳

Cooking Time: 20 minutes ✳

Time-Saving Tip: Cook the onions and mushrooms in one pan while browning the meat in another pan. ✳

Hamburger Stroganoff sounds a little odd because Stroganoff sounds fancy while hamburger does not. This recipe is actually an adaptation of beef stroganoff, with ground beef substituted for sliced beef. Calling the whole dish Ground Beef Stroganoff would be confusing, as it implies that you make Beef Stroganoff and then put it into a blender (as if preparing it for a baby to eat). Hence, Hamburger Stroganoff. It's much faster to prepare with ground beef, and tastes just as good. It just doesn't sound as fancy.

1 large onion

2 tablespoons olive or corn oil

1/2 pound presliced mushrooms

1 teaspoon bottled crushed garlic

1 teaspoon salt

1/2 teaspoon black pepper

1 pound lean ground beef (see Mom Tip)

1 cup sour cream

1 tablespoon ketchup

1 teaspoon Dijon mustard

1 teaspoon Worcestershire sauce

Peel the onion and cut it into 1/2-inch pieces. Put the oil into a large frying pan or wok and begin heating over medium-high heat. Add the onion and cook, stirring occasionally, about 5 minutes, or until it has begun to soften. Add the mushrooms, garlic, salt and black pepper and cook about 5 minutes, or until the mushrooms soften. Transfer the onions/mushroom mixture and any juices to a plate and then set aside.

Add the ground beef to the pan, breaking it up into small chunks, and let it brown for 5 minutes over medium-high heat, stirring occasionally. Drain and discard the fat.

Put the onion/mushroom mixture back into the pan with the meat. Add the sour cream, ketchup, mustard and Worcestershire sauce and stir. Bring the mixture to a boil, cover and turn down to medium-low heat. Cook for 10 minutes, stirring occasionally. Serve immediately. Or set aside until ready to eat, and then reheat briefly.

Mom Tip: You can substitute ground turkey or ground pork.

Indian-Style Lamb Kebabs

Serves: 4 ✳

Preparation time: 15 minutes ✳

Cooking time: 8 minutes ✳

Time-saving tip: Use 2 tablespoons garam masala (see Mom Tip 1 with Chicken Tikka, page 147) in place of the ginger, cumin, coriander, cinnamon, cloves and nutmeg. ✳

I don't tend to eat much lamb, probably because of the good publicity the cute critters got in nursery rhymes. But these kebabs, made from ground lamb and a combination of Indian spices, taste too good to pass up. Maybe I'll write a poem about them. Now, what rhymes with kebab?

1 medium onion

1 1/2 pounds ground lamb or beef

2 tablespoons bottled lemon juice

2 teaspoons bottled crushed garlic

2 teaspoons bottled ginger or 1 teaspoon ground ginger

1 teaspoon ground cumin

1 teaspoon ground coriander

1/2 teaspoon ground cinnamon

1/2 teaspoon ground cloves

1/2 teaspoon ground nutmeg

1/2 teaspoon salt

1/2 teaspoon black pepper

Dash cayenne pepper

8 skewers

Pita bread (optional)

Preheat the broiler. Make sure the top oven rack is in the highest position, just under the broiling unit. For easy clean-up, line the broiling pan with aluminum foil. Place the broiling pan rack on top of the foil and then set aside (see Mom Warning).

Peel the onion and cut it into eighths. Put the onion, lamb or beef, lemon juice, garlic, ginger, cumin, coriander, cinnamon, cloves, nutmeg, salt, black pepper and cayenne pepper into the bowl of a food processor and process about 1 minute, or until the mixture is smooth and pastelike. Divide into eight equal portions.

Wet your hands and pat the portions into 6 inch cylindrical shapes. Gently thread a skewer through the middle of each shape and lay the filled skewers onto the broiling pan rack. Broil for 4 minutes per side, or until the kebabs have begun to brown and are firm to the touch. Serve immediately. Or set aside until ready to eat, and then reheat briefly. If using pita bread, wrap a bread around each skewer and gently pull the lamb off the skewer and eat as a sandwich.

Mom Warning: If you don't use the rack, the meat will cook in its own juices and will be mushy.

Steve's Picadillo

Serves: 4 ✳

Preparation time: 5 minutes ✳

Cooking time: 20 minutes ✳

Time-saving tip: Use frozen chopped onions and bell pepper slices. ✳

"Picadillo" may sound like a musical instrument played by a fairy tale prince, but I assure you that our family friend Steve Riskin, who gave us this recipe, would never play such an instrument. Picadillo is actually a Cuban-style Sloppy Joe. It's big, messy, and worth it. Put on a bib and dig in.

1 medium onion

1 medium red bell pepper

1 tablespoon olive or corn oil

2 slices precooked bacon (see Mom Tip)

1 pound lean ground beef

1 teaspoon bottled crushed garlic

1 teaspoon salt

1/2 teaspoon black pepper

1/2 teaspoon ground cumin

1/2 teaspoon dried oregano

1/2 teaspoon paprika

1/8 teaspoon cayenne pepper

1/2 cup pimiento-stuffed green olives, sliced or whole

1/2 cup raisins

1 8-ounce can tomato sauce

Peel the onion. Rinse the bell pepper, cut it in half and remove and discard the stem and seeds. Cut the onion and bell pepper into 1/2-inch pieces. Put the oil into a large, heavy-bottomed frying pan and begin heating over medium-high heat. Add the onion and bell pepper and cook about 5 minutes, stirring occasionally, or until the vegetables begin to soften. Transfer to a plate. While the vegetables are cooking, cut the precooked bacon into 1-inch pieces and then set aside.

Add the ground beef to the pan, breaking it up into small chunks, and let it brown for 5 minutes, stirring occasionally. Drain and discard the fat. Return the onion and bell pepper to the pan. Add the garlic, salt, black pepper, cumin, oregano, paprika, cayenne pepper, precooked bacon, olives, raisins and tomato sauce and mix well.

Bring the mixture to a boil, cover and turn down to medium heat. Cook for 10 minutes, stirring occasionally. If the mixture seems too dry, add 1/4 cup water. Serve over rice or noodles or on a bun or a tortilla.

Mom Tip: Instead of bacon, I sometimes use 2 or 3 slices of prosciutto, cut into 1/2-inch pieces.

Sausages, Onions and Peppers

Serves: 4 ✳

Preparation time: 10 minutes ✳

Cooking time: 20 minutes (cooking and preparation times overlap) ✳

Time-saving tip: Use cooked sausages cut into 1-inch slices. ✳

This is a very English dish. The English may have lost their empire, but that plucky little island country, land of my birth and home to my heart, will always know how to cook sausages. Sausages, Onions and Peppers is the perfect meal to eat after a long rainy day, whether you're a queen or a chimney sweep.

1 1/2 pounds uncooked sausages (see Mom Tip)

2 large onions

2 large red, yellow or green bell peppers

3 tablespoons olive or corn oil

1 teaspoon salt

1/2 teaspoon black pepper

Put the sausages into a large pot and cover them with water. Bring to a boil over high heat. Turn down to medium-high heat and cook, uncovered, for 10 minutes. Drain the sausages, return them to the pot and cook over medium-high heat about 4 minutes, or until they start to brown. Move them around with a wooden spoon or spatula so they don't stick. Remove from heat and cut the sausages into 1-inch rings with a knife or kitchen scissors.

While the sausages are cooking, peel the onions. Rinse the bell peppers, cut them in half and remove and discard the stems and seeds. Cut the onions and bell peppers into 1/2-inch slices.

Put the oil into a wok or large frying pan and begin heating over medium-high heat. Add the onions, bell peppers, salt and black pepper and cook about 10 minutes, stirring occasionally, or until they are very soft.

Add the cooked sausages and stir about 1 minute, or until the mixture is hot. Serve immediately. Or set aside until ready to eat, and then reheat briefly.

Mom Tip: I prefer hot Italian sausages, but there are many choices, including variously flavored turkey and chicken sausages.

Short-Cut Beef Bourguignon

Serves: 4 ✳

Preparation time: 15 minutes ✳

Cooking time: 7 minutes ✳

Time-saving tip: Use drained whole or sliced canned mushrooms. ✳

I actually believe that the short-cut version of Beef Bourguignon tastes better than the traditional wait-half-a-lifetime, need-to-shave-twice-while-cooking version. What recipe wouldn't be improved by adding sirloin steak? If I could, I'd add sirloin steak to my breakfast cereal.

1 14 1/2-ounce jar whole baby onions

1/2 cup red wine

1 10-ounce can condensed beef broth OR 2 beef bouillon cubes, 2 teaspoons
    beef bouillon granules or 2 teaspoons beef base plus 1 1/4 cups water

1 tablespoon tomato paste or ketchup

1 teaspoon bottled crushed garlic

1 bay leaf

1/2 teaspoon dried thyme

1/4 teaspoon black pepper

1 1/2 pounds sirloin steak (see Mom Tip)

2 tablespoons olive or corn oil

1 pound presliced mushrooms

Drain the bottled onions and discard the liquid. Put the onions, wine, beef broth, tomato paste or ketchup, garlic, bay leaf, thyme and black pepper into a medium pot and bring to a boil over high heat. Remove from heat, cover and then set aside.

Cut off and discard any visible fat on the beef and slice the meat into strips 1/2 inch wide and 2 inches long.

Put 1 tablespoon of the oil into a wok or large frying pan and begin heating over high heat. Add the steak strips and stir-fry for 3 minutes, or until they are no longer pink. Transfer the meat to a plate and then set aside. Add the remaining tablespoon oil to the wok or frying pan and stir-fry the mushrooms about 3 minutes, or until they begin to brown. Remove from heat, drain and discard any mushroom liquid.

Add the onion mixture and the meat to the mushrooms and heat over medium-high heat about 1 minute, or until hot. Remove and discard the bay leaf. Serve immediately or set aside until ready to eat, and then reheat briefly.

Mom Tip: In addition to sirloin steak, you can use any steak that you would broil or grill, including New York strip, shell, T-bone, porterhouse, rib, rib eye or Delmonico. Do not buy chuck or round steak or stewing beef for this recipe because those cuts require longer cooking.

Sweet and Sour Pork with Broccoli

Serves: 4 ✳

Preparation time: 15 minutes ✳

Cooking time: 10 minutes ✳

Time-saving tip: Buy precut fresh broccoli in a bag. ✳

To me, "sweet and sour" are magic words. I know I'm going to like something if it's sweet and sour. Sweet and sour rutabaga would probably be more than edible. But there's no doubt about Sweet and Sour Pork with Broccoli. I should know—I've eaten it more than a hundred times. It's a recipe I grew up with. When I cook it, it tastes almost as good as when my mom cooks it. How do moms do that?

1 pound boneless pork chops

3 tablespoons soy sauce, divided

2 teaspoons cornstarch

1 large onion

1/2 pound broccoli (about 3 cups)

2 tablespoons peanut or corn oil plus more if needed

1/4 teaspoon red pepper flakes

1/4 cup sugar

1/4 cup ketchup

1/4 cup white vinegar

Trim and discard any visible fat from the pork. Cut the pork into strips 1/4 inch wide and 2 inches long and put them into a medium bowl. Add 2 tablespoons of the soy sauce and the cornstarch and stir until the cornstarch dissolves and then set aside.

Peel the onion and cut it into 1/2-inch pieces. Rinse the broccoli. Trim and discard any leaves and the bottom 1 inch of the stem(s). Peel and discard 1/4 inch of the tough outer surface of the stem(s). Slice the remaining stem(s) into 1/4-inch discs. Cut the florets into bite-size pieces.

Put 1 tablespoon of the oil into a wok or large frying pan and begin heating over medium-high heat. Add the red pepper flakes, onion and broccoli and stir-fry about 3 minutes, or until the vegetables just begin to soften. Transfer them to a plate and add the remaining tablespoon of oil to the pan.

Add the pork and any juices and stir-fry about 3 minutes, or until the pork has browned on all sides. Add the sugar, ketchup, vinegar and remaining tablespoon soy sauce and bring the mixture to a boil. The liquid will thicken and look shiny. Return the vegetables to the pork mixture and continue cooking, stirring frequently, about 1 minute, or until the mixture is hot. Serve immediately or set aside until ready to eat, and then reheat briefly.

Chinese-Style Pork Medallions

Serves: 4

Preparation time: 15 minutes

Cooking time: 10 minutes

Time-saving tip: Use two frying pans so you can cook more at once.

This is one of the recipes I would always ask mom to cook growing up. It seemed like the height of luxury. When I'd come home from college, this is what I wanted. I was a little disillusioned when I found out how easy it was to make. It was sort of like meeting your favorite movie star and finding out that he's actually five-foot two. But I got over my shock, and now I'm glad it's so simple. I still sometimes ask my mom to cook it though.

1/2 cup cider vinegar

1/2 cup water

1/3 cup apricot preserves or plum jam

2 tablespoons sugar

2 tablespoons soy sauce

1 tablespoon cornstarch

1/4 teaspoon black pepper

1 to 1 1/2 pounds pork tenderloin

1 tablespoon peanut or corn oil plus more if needed

Put the vinegar, water, apricot preserves or plum jam, sugar, soy sauce, cornstarch and black pepper into a small bowl and mix well and then set aside.

Trim any fat from the tenderloin and slice it into 12 pieces, each about 1 inch thick. Put these pieces between sheets of wax paper and pound them to 1/4-inch thickness with a rolling pin or the side of a can.

Put 1 tablespoon of the oil into a wok or large frying pan and begin heating over medium-high heat. Add half the pork medallions and cook about 2 minutes per side, or until they have lost their pink color. Transfer them to a plate and cook the remaining pork medallions, adding more oil if necessary. Transfer them to the plate.

Add the vinegar mixture to the wok or frying pan and bring to a boil. Return the pork medallions to the pan, and then reheat briefly. Serve immediately or just before you are ready to eat, reheat the pork medallions in the sauce.

Quick-Fried Pork Chops

Serves: 4 ✳

Preparation time: 10 minutes ✳

Cooking time: 8 minutes ✳

Time-saving tip: Use precooked asparagus from the grocery store's salad bar. ✳

Pork chops used to be part of the weekly American dinner rotation, along with such mainstays as meat loaf and macaroni and cheese. But time passed, and chicken, beef and fish (not to mention vegetarianism) muscled pork chops onto the sidelines. Perhaps this recipe will bring them back. With added flavors like ginger, honey, vinegar and soy sauce, these aren't your grandmother's pork chops.

1 bunch scallions or 1/2 pound asparagus

4 boneless pork loin chops (about 1 1/2 pounds)

1 tablespoon peanut or corn oil

1 tablespoon bottled ginger or 1 teaspoon ground ginger

1 teaspoon bottled crushed garlic

1/4 teaspoon red pepper flakes

1/4 teaspoon black pepper

1/4 cup white vinegar

2 tablespoons honey

2 tablespoons soy sauce

2 teaspoons water

1 teaspoon cornstarch

Rinse and trim the scallions or asparagus and cut into 2-inch pieces and then set aside.

Trim any fat from the pork chops. Flatten them between sheets of wax paper, using a rolling pin or heavy can, to 1/4-inch thickness and then set aside.

Put the oil into a large frying pan and begin heating over medium-high heat. Add the ginger, garlic, red pepper flakes and black pepper and cook about 30 seconds, or until the ginger and garlic begin to sizzle. Add the pork chops and cook about 1 minute per side, or until they have lost their pink color. Add the vinegar, honey and soy sauce, stir and bring the mixture to a boil. Add the scallions or asparagus and mix gently. Cover, turn down to low heat and cook about 5 minutes, or until the chops are no longer pink in the middle.

Put the water and cornstarch into a small cup, stir until the cornstarch dissolves and add to the pork chop sauce. Bring the mixture to a boil so that it will thicken slightly. Serve immediately or set aside until ready to eat, and then reheat briefly.

Spicy Skirt Steak

Serves: 4

Preparation time: 10 minutes *

Cooking time: 4 minutes *

Time-saving tip: Use a prepackaged spice mixture. *

Once on a cross-country drive as a kid my family stopped at a restaurant in Texas that offered a free 72-ounce steak, provided you ate it all in one sitting. I begged my parents to let me try. They said absolutely not and bought me a balloon instead. It was a very quiet dinner.

Now that I'm older, I realize that a person probably shouldn't eat 72 ounces of steak in a month, let alone in one bloated gorge-out. But once in a while it's a real treat. Spicy Skirt Steak is what I would serve aliens to show them how good Earth food can be.

1 to 1 1/2 pounds skirt steak or flank steak (see Mom Tip 1)

1 teaspoon sugar

1 teaspoon salt

1 teaspoon black pepper

1/2 teaspoon garlic powder

1/2 teaspoon ground coriander

1/2 teaspoon paprika

2 tablespoons olive or corn oil

Trim and discard any visible fat. Cut the skirt steak into 4 pieces. If using flank steak, keep it whole.

Put the sugar, salt, black pepper, garlic powder, ground coriander and paprika into a cup and mix well.

Sprinkle 1/2 the spice mixture on one side of the steak and press it in with the back of a spoon.

Put the oil into a large frying pan, grill pan or griddle and begin heating over medium-high heat about 1 minute, or until a drop of water flicked into the pan sizzles. Add the steak to the pan, spiced side down, and cook for 2 minutes.

Sprinkle the rest of the spice mixture on the top of the steak and press it in with the back of a spoon. Turn the meat over and cook it another 2 minutes. Cut into the center to see how cooked it is. If it's too rare, cook 1 minute more or even longer. But remember that the meat will continue cooking after you take it out of the pan. Don't cook beyond medium rare or the steak will be tough.

Remove the steak from the pan and let it rest on a cutting board for 2 minutes. Slice the meat thinly at a 45-degree angle across the fibers (see Mom Tip 2) and serve immediately.

Mom Tip 1: Skirt steak is a long, flat boneless piece of beef that almost looks striped because of the prominent fibers. It can be cooked quickly, but in order to be tender, rather than stringy, it must be cut across the fibers rather than between the fibers. Flank steak, which is a different cut of meat, has the same stripy look and can be cooked the same way.

Mom Tip 2: If the meat seems too rare once it's cut, slip it back into the pan and cook it a few seconds more.

Easy Veal Chops

Serves: 4 ✳

Preparation time: 2 minutes ✳

Cooking time: 6 minutes ✳

Time-saving tip: Pound the veal chops to 1/2-inch thickness and cook about 4 minutes total. ✳

I have two food-related memories of a trip to Paris I took several years ago. The first is of a waiter with no respect for my personal space who asked me, with our noses almost touching, if I would like some cheese. The other is of delicious veal chops I had at a fancy restaurant called Au Pied du Cochon. While only in France would a high-class eatery be named after a pig's foot, the food was good enough to make up for any name. My mom was there too and was inspired to create this easy recipe.

  1 tablespoon olive or corn oil

  1 tablespoon butter

  4 veal loin or rib chops, about 3/4 inch thick

  1/2 cup chicken broth

  1/2 teaspoon salt

  1/4 teaspoon black pepper

Put the oil and butter into a large frying pan or wok and begin heating over medium-high heat. When the butter has melted, add the veal chops and cook 2 minutes per side, or until both sides have slightly browned. Add the chicken broth, salt and black pepper and cook about 2 minutes, or until the liquid has thickened slightly. The veal will be pink in the center. Serve immediately or set aside until ready to eat, and then reheat briefly.

Mom Tip: One veal chop per person is enough for a meal. Loin chops are slightly more tender than rib chops and are more expensive. Both can be successfully cooked in about 6 minutes.

Beef Teriyaki

Serves: 4 ✳

Preparation time: 19 minutes ✳

Cooking time: 4–6 minutes ✳

Time-saving tip: Use 2/3 cup bottled teriyaki sauce instead of making your own. ✳

Every year in my adopted hometown of Manhattan Beach, California, there is a 10K race, followed by a fair with lots of great food and booths for kids to throw their money down the drain. I've made it a habit to run the race and reward myself with a few sticks of Beef Teriyaki. Up until recently, this was the only time during the year I would eat it, and boy was it good. But now that I've learned how to make it myself, I've lost all interest in jogging. I hope learning this recipe won't have the same impact on your exercise program.

1 to 1 1/2 pounds sirloin steak at least 1 inch thick

1/2 cup soy sauce

1/4 cup brown sugar

2 tablespoons olive or corn oil

2 teaspoons bottled ginger or 1 teaspoon ground ginger

1 teaspoon bottled crushed garlic

1/2 teaspoon black pepper

Skewers

Preheat the broiler. Make sure the top oven rack is in the highest position, just under the broiling unit. For easy clean-up, line the broiling pan with aluminum foil and place the broiling pan rack on top of the foil and then set aside. Or heat up your gas grill.

Trim all visible fat from the beef and cut it into strips 6 to 8 inches long and 1/4 inch thick. To make the Teriyaki Sauce, put the soy sauce, brown sugar, oil, ginger, garlic and black pepper into a medium bowl and mix well. Add the beef and stir, making sure the marinade covers all the meat's surfaces and then set aside on the counter for 5 minutes.

Thread the beef onto the skewers so that each strip is pierced 3 or 4 times and looks like a double S shape. Discard the leftover marinade. When the broiler or grill is ready, cook the skewers about 2 minutes per side (medium rare) or 3 minutes per side (medium).

Serve immediately on the skewers.

Grilled Steak Slices

Serves: 4 ✳

Preparation time: 10 minutes ✳

Cooking time: 16–20 minutes (preparation and cooking times overlap)

Time-saving tip: Use 1-inch-thick steak and cook for 4–5 minutes per side. ✳

This recipe comes from my parents' neighbor, Mary Morigaki. Their houses are pretty close, and when I was growing up I could smell what she was cooking for dinner, as well as hear her singing along to the *Cats* soundtrack. She's a great cook, as this recipe demonstrates. So, be sure to cook with the windows open. Choose your own music.

1 to 1 1/2 pounds sirloin steak, about 1 1/2 inches thick

1 tablespoon olive or corn oil

1 teaspoon salt

1/2 teaspoon black pepper

1 6-ounce bag prewashed arugula (see Mom Tip)

1 small red onion

Chunk fresh Parmesan cheese

Preheat the broiler. Make sure the top oven rack is 5–6 inches under the broiling unit. For easy clean-up, line the broiling pan with aluminum foil. Place the broiling pan rack on top of the foil and then set aside. Or heat up your gas grill.

Trim and discard any visible fat from the steak. Brush both sides of the steak with oil and sprinkle with salt and black pepper. When the broiler or grill is ready, cook the steak about 8 minutes per side (medium rare) or 10 minutes per side (medium).

While the steak is cooking, distribute the arugula onto four plates. Peel the red onion and cut it into 1/8-inch slices and then set aside. With a sharp knife, shave 12 thin slices of Parmesan cheese from the chunk and then set aside. Wrap and refrigerate the rest of the cheese for another use.

As soon as the steak is cooked, transfer it to a cutting board and slice it into 1/4-inch slices. Place the slices and any juices on top of each plate of arugula. Top with a few slices of red onion and 3 slices of shaved Parmesan cheese. Serve immediately.

Mom Tip: Arugula, which has a slightly bitter taste, offers a strong contrast with the steak. If you can't find arugula, use some escarole leaves or mixed salad greens.

Lamb Souvlakia

Serves: 4 ✳

Preparation time: 15 minutes ✳

Cooking time: 8–10 minutes ✳

Time-saving tip: Buy precut lamb. ✳

When my mom was a teenager she was an exchange student in Greece. I used to ask her what Plato and Aristotle were like in person. She would smile and tell me that she couldn't get to first base with Plato, and Aristotle should have invented toothpaste while he was being brilliant. So she may not have returned to America with her head full of profound wisdom learned from the ancient masters, but she was laden with recipes. This is one of them. She says "souvla" is the Greek word for skewer.

1 1/2 pounds boneless lamb

3 tablespoons olive oil

2 tablespoons bottled lemon juice

1 teaspoon bottled crushed garlic

1 teaspoon dried oregano

1/2 teaspoon salt

1/2 teaspoon black pepper

Skewers

4 pita breads (optional)

Preheat the broiler. Make sure the top oven rack is 5–6 inches under the broiling unit. For easy clean-up, line the broiling pan with aluminum foil. Place the broiling pan rack on top of the foil and then set aside. Or heat up your gas grill.

Trim all visible fat from the lamb and cut it into 1-inch cubes. Put the olive oil, lemon juice, garlic, oregano, salt and black pepper into a medium bowl and mix well. Add the lamb and stir, making sure the marinade covers all the meat's surfaces, and then set aside on the counter for 5 minutes.

Thread the lamb onto the skewers, leaving at least 1/4 inch of space between each piece so the lamb will cook more quickly. Discard the marinade. When the broiler or grill is ready, cook the lamb skewers for 4 minutes per side (medium rare) or 5 minutes per side (medium).

Serve immediately. If using pita bread, wrap a bread around each skewer and gently pull the lamb off the skewer and eat as a sandwich. Or you can serve over Toasted Barley (page 226).

Roast Beef in 20 Minutes

Serves: 6–8 ✳

Preparation time: 5 minutes ✳

Cooking time: 15 minutes ✳

Time-saving tip: Don't let roast sit after cooking. ✳

Normally roast beef takes more than an hour to cook, but by turning the knob on your oven all the way to the right you can cut that time in half. I suppose you could cook it even faster in a kiln, but very few people have those lying around. This simple technique goes against all the traditional cookbook rules but saves time without sacrificing taste.

> **1 1/2- to 2-pound beef tri-tip roast** (see Mom Tip 1)
>
> **Salt**
>
> **Black pepper**
>
> **Horseradish Sauce or Spicy Peanut Sauce** (optional) (see recipes on next page)

Place one of the oven racks in the middle position and preheat the oven to 475 degrees F. For easy clean-up, line the broiling pan with aluminum foil. Place the broiling pan rack on top of the foil and then set aside.

Cut the roast in half crosswise through the middle so that you have 2 large slabs, each about 3/4 inch thick. Season with salt and black pepper and place on the broiling pan rack, cut side down.

When the oven is ready, cook the meat for 15 minutes. It will be medium-rare. Remove from heat, trim away fat and slice thinly. Serve immediately. The pieces will be smaller than you are accustomed to with roast beef, but the taste will be the same.

Horseradish Sauce

1/4 cup sour cream

2 teaspoons bottled horseradish

1 teaspoon bottled lemon juice

Put the sour cream, horseradish and lemon juice into a small bowl and mix well.

Spicy Peanut Sauce

2/3 cup milk plus more if necessary

1/2 cup peanut butter plus more
   if necessary

2 tablespoons soy sauce

1 tablespoon bottled lemon juice

1 teaspoon bottled crushed garlic

1 teaspoon sesame oil

1/2 teaspoon ground ginger

1/4 teaspoon red pepper flakes

Put all the ingredients into a small pot, mix well and bring to a boil over high heat, continuing to stir. If the sauce seems too thick, add more milk, a tablespoon at a time, and stir until it is as thin as you want it. If it's too thin, add more peanut butter, a tablespoon at a time, and stir until it is as thick as you want it.

Mom Tip 1: A tri-tip roast (also known as a triangle roast or bottom sirloin butt) is a thin, relatively small cut of beef. Tri-tip is roughly triangular in shape and about 1 1/2 inches thick. A rib-eye roast, which is also boneless, can be substituted for a tri-tip. Depending on its size, you may have to slice it into 3 or 4 slabs, each about 3/4 inch thick.

Mom Tip 2: Use leftovers for Philly Steak Sandwiches (page 60).

183

Roast Pork Tenderloin

Serves: 4–6 ✳

Preparation time: 5 minutes ✳

Cooking time: 20 minutes ✳

Time-saving tip: Smaller pork tenderloins cook faster. ✳

Pork tenderloin may be more expensive than other cuts, but it's worth it. It's boneless, tender (hence the name), and quick to cook. If you've never prepared this other white meat before, give it a try. You'll be surprised how easy it is.

1/2 cup honey

1/4 cup brown sugar

1/4 cup cider vinegar

2 teaspoons dry mustard

2 pork tenderloins (about 1 pound each)

Place an oven rack in the middle position and preheat the oven to 475 degrees F. For easy clean-up, line a baking sheet with aluminum foil.

Put the honey, brown sugar, vinegar and dry mustard into a small pot and mix well and then set aside.

Trim any fat from the tenderloins. Place the tenderloins on the foil and spoon a few tablespoons of the honey mixture over top. Bake for 10 minutes. Turn the tenderloins over, spoon a few more tablespoons of the honey mixture over top and bake another 10 minutes.

Near the end of the cooking time, bring the remaining honey mixture to a boil and keep hot over low heat.

Slice the tenderloins into 1/2-inch slices and serve with hot honey sauce.

Untraditional Veal Parmesan

Serves: 4

Preparation time: 5 minutes

Cooking time: 5–10 minutes

Time-saving tip: Use two frying pans to cook all the veal at once.

My mother tells me that when she would go on road trips as a child in the 1950s, they would stop every night at Howard Johnson's so my grandfather could order Veal Parmesan. Apparently he was stuck in quite a deep gastronomic rut. But I understand. Veal Parmesan can be addictive. My mother's brother Steve altered the formula slightly, replacing the traditional mozzarella with muenster cheese. Hopefully my grandfather would have approved.

4 thinly sliced veal cutlets (about 1 to 1 1/4 pounds) (see Mom Tip)

1 tablespoon olive oil plus more if needed

1 cup marinara sauce plus more if serving with pasta

4 1-ounce slices muenster cheese

1/4 cup grated Parmesan cheese

Trim and discard any visible fat from the veal.

Put the oil into a large frying pan or wok and begin heating over medium-high heat. Add as many slices of veal as will fit in the pan and cook for 2 minutes per side, or until both sides have slightly browned. Spoon 1/4 cup marinara sauce over each cutlet and lay a slice of muenster cheese on top. Sprinkle 1 tablespoon Parmesan cheese on each slice of muenster. Cover the pan and cook about 1 minute, or until the muenster melts. Serve immediately. Repeat the process until all the veal is cooked. If you are serving this dish with plain pasta, heat the remaining marinara sauce and either spoon some over the pasta or offer it in a serving bowl.

Mom Tip: Veal cutlets, also sold as veal scallops or veal scallopini, are thin, boneless slices of veal. They are very tender and cook quickly, but they are expensive. You can substitute boneless chicken breasts in this recipe as long as you slice or pound the breasts to 1/4-inch thickness.

Fish & Shellfish

I have some long-standing hang-ups about cooking fish. I worry about buying the wrong thing, I worry about removing bones and skin, and I worry about making sure it's cooked all the way through. So in this section we've made sure to address these issues. Now I'm much more comfortable cooking recipes like Easy Baked Salmon, Sole Florentine and Pan-Fried Trout. At last, it's safe to go into the water.

Deviled Salmon Patties

Easy Baked Salmon

Catfish Masala

Pan-Fried Trout

Sole Florentine

Almost Crab Cakes

Coconut Shrimp Curry

Scallop Kebabs

Stir-Fried Scampi

Deviled Salmon Patties

Serves: 4 ✳

Preparation time: 10–15 minutes ✳

Cooking time: 8 minutes ✳

Time-saving tip: Use boneless canned salmon. The extra cost is worth the convenience. ✳

Salmon patties are a great alternative way to eat fish. They're very easy to prepare, particularly if you use the boneless, skinless salmon. The fact that they're "deviled" doesn't mean that they're from a dark underworld. "Deviled" merely means that something is cooked with hot or spicy condiments, in this case, mustard.

4 scallions

1 small red bell pepper

4 6-ounce cans boneless, skinless salmon or 2 14 1/2-ounce cans red or pink salmon

1/2 cup sour cream

1 cup seasoned bread crumbs, divided, plus more if needed

2 tablespoons Dijon mustard

1 teaspoon Worcestershire sauce

1/2 teaspoon salt

1/4 teaspoon black pepper

1/8 teaspoon cayenne pepper

1 tablespoon butter plus more if needed

1 tablespoon olive or corn oil plus more if needed

Tartar Sauce (see Mom Tip)

Rinse and trim the scallions, and cut them into 1/2-inch pieces. Rinse the bell pepper, cut in half, remove and discard the stem and seeds and cut into 1/2-inch pieces.

If using boneless salmon, put it into a medium bowl and add the scallions, bell pepper, sour cream, 1/2 cup of the bread crumbs, mustard, Worcestershire sauce, salt, black pepper and cayenne pepper.

If using regular cans of salmon, drain and discard the liquid. Remove and discard all skin and bones and separate the salmon into flakes and proceed as above.

Mix the ingredients together and shape into eight large, flat patties. Put the remaining 1/2 cup seasoned bread crumbs onto a large plate and press both sides of each patty into the crumbs, adding more crumbs if needed.

Put the butter and oil into a large frying pan and begin heating over medium-high heat. When the butter is melted, add as many patties as will fit in the pan and cook about 2 minutes on each side, or until the crumbs are brown and the patties are hot. Serve immediately or transfer to a plate and keep warm in the oven while cooking the rest of the patties, adding more butter and oil as needed.

Mom Tip: Tartar sauce is available in bottles in the mayonnaise or gourmet food aisle. To make your own tartar sauce, combine 1/4 cup mayonnaise with 2 tablespoons sweet relish in a small dish.

Easy Baked Salmon

Serves: 4 ✳

Preparation time: 5 minutes ✳

Cooking time: 10 minutes ✳

Time-saving tip: Cut salmon into four serving-size pieces. It will cook faster. ✳

How great is it that you can buy boneless salmon? It removes the one great impediment to cooking fish. True, you have to make sure the bones are all gone, but the process is so much easier. Easy Baked Salmon is the perfect recipe for people who aren't used to cooking fish and want a simple and tasty introduction.

1 boneless salmon fillet (1 1/2 to 2 pounds)

1 small onion

1 lemon

Garlic Mayonnaise (see Mom Tip)

Place an oven rack in the middle position and preheat the oven to 425 degrees F. Line a baking sheet with aluminum foil for easy cleanup.

Rinse the salmon and check it for bones. Sometimes there are a few near the edges or right in the center. Remove and discard any you find. Pat the salmon dry with paper towels and lay it, skin side down, on the baking sheet.

Peel the onion and cut it into 1/4-inch slices. Rinse the lemon and cut it into paper-thin slices. Scatter the onion and lemon slices on top of the salmon.

Bake about 10 minutes, or until the salmon just begins to flake. Remove from oven and, using a knife, cut the fillet into four servings. Slip a metal spatula between the salmon and the skin and gently slide the first serving onto a plate, leaving the skin on the foil. Repeat until all the salmon has been served. Serve with Garlic Mayonnaise, if desired. This salmon is also good cold.

Mom Tip: Garlic Mayonnaise is very easy to make. Combine 1/2 cup mayonnaise with 1 teaspoon bottled crushed garlic and 1/2 teaspoon dried dill in a small dish.

Catfish Masala

Serves: 4

Preparation time: 10 minutes

Cooking time: 15 minutes

Time-saving tip: Use frozen chopped onions and frozen bell pepper slices.

Some women gossip at the hairdresser. My mom and her hairdresser, Ruki, discuss recipes. The recipes Ruki provides, like this one, are mostly from her native Lahore region in Pakistan, and they're always good. Hopefully Ruki likes the recipes mom gives her in return. I'd hate for mom to come back one day with a rainbow-colored mohawk.

1 1/2 pounds catfish, red snapper or tilapia

1 medium onion

1 large tomato

1 medium green bell pepper

2 tablespoons olive or corn oil

1 teaspoon bottled crushed garlic

1 teaspoon bottled ginger or 1/2 teaspoon ground ginger

1 teaspoon paprika

1 teaspoon ground coriander

1/2 teaspoon ground cumin

1/2 teaspoon ground turmeric

1/2 teaspoon salt

1/8 teaspoon cayenne pepper

Cut the fish into 2-inch pieces. Peel the onion and cut it into 1/4-inch slices. Rinse the tomato. Rinse the bell pepper, cut it in half and remove and discard the stem and seeds. Cut the tomato and bell pepper into 1/2-inch pieces. Then set the vegetables aside.

Put 1 tablespoon of the oil into a large frying pan or wok and begin heating over medium-high heat. Add the fish and cook for 5 minutes, stirring occasionally. Remove from heat and transfer the fish and any liquid to a bowl.

Add the remaining tablespoon oil to the pan and begin heating over medium-high heat. Add the onion, tomato and bell pepper and cook about 5 minutes, stirring occasionally, or until the vegetables begin to soften. Add the garlic, ginger, paprika, coriander, cumin, turmeric, salt and cayenne pepper and mix well. Return the partly cooked fish to the pan and stir gently so it is covered with sauce. Turn down to medium heat, cover and cook for 5 minutes.

Serve immediately or set aside until ready to eat, and then reheat briefly.

Pan-Fried Trout

Serves: 4 ✳

Preparation time: 5 minutes ✳

Cooking time: 8–10 minutes ✳

Time-saving tip: If you don't plan to eat the skin, don't bother coating the trout with cornmeal or flour. ✳

I'm not outdoorsy by nature. If I were put in a survival situation, I would probably munch on some wild berries, go mad and try to flap my arms really fast and fly away. Thank goodness the odds are against my having to rely on my wits to live. Luckily for me, I live in the time of supermarkets. I can go and buy a trout, precleaned, bring it home and fry it up. It sure tastes good in my climate-controlled house.

4 cleaned trout (about 3/4 pound each)

1/2 cup cornmeal or flour

1/2 teaspoon salt

1/4 teaspoon black pepper

1/8 teaspoon cayenne pepper (optional)

2 tablespoons olive oil or butter

4 lemon halves

Rinse the trout in cold running water, making sure all the insides have been cleaned out, and then set aside. Put the cornmeal or flour, salt, black pepper and cayenne pepper, if using, into a large paper bag and shake.

Put the olive oil or butter into a large frying pan or wok and begin heating over medium-high heat. When it is hot, put a trout into the paper bag, hold it closed and shake it several times to coat the trout with the mixture. Put the trout in the pan and repeat the process with the remaining trout. Cook for 4–5 minutes per side, or until the coating has browned and the fish has turned white. Pull up a piece of the skin to check.

Serve immediately, providing 1 lemon half per person. Advise diners to eat the top layer of fish (and skin, if desired) and then gently pull away and discard the backbone. Then they can eat the bottom layer.

Sole Florentine

Serves: 4 ✳

Preparation time: 5 minutes plus 4 minutes for Garlicky Spinach ✳

Cooking time: 15 minutes ✳

Time-saving tip: Use two frying pans to poach all the fish at once. ✳

There's a general feeling, and I have it frequently myself, that if a dish sounds fancy it must be difficult to make. Sole Florentine has that sound. If I saw it on a restaurant menu, I would assume that you had to go to school for many years to learn how to make it. But that's not true. Sole is simple to buy and simple to prepare. And "Florentine" merely means "with spinach." So, in a few steps you can skip all that schooling and make yourself a very good plate of fish.

2 tablespoons butter or olive oil

2 tablespoons flour

1 cup milk

1 teaspoon bottled lemon juice

1 tablespoon grated Parmesan cheese

1/2 teaspoon salt

1/4 teaspoon black pepper

1 1/2 pounds sole fillets (or flounder or tilapia, also about 1/4 inch thick)

Water

Garlicky Spinach (see page 212)

1/2 cup seasoned bread crumbs

Preheat the broiler. Make sure the top oven rack is in the highest position, just under the broiling unit. Wipe a baking sheet with a bit of oil or use a nonstick sheet and then set aside.

Put the butter or oil into a small pot and begin heating over medium-high heat. When the butter is melted or the oil is hot, add the flour and stir until well combined. Add the milk and lemon juice and stir with a whisk about 2 minutes, or until the mixture thickens and has no lumps. Add the Parmesan cheese, salt and black pepper and continue stirring until the cheese melts. Remove from heat and then set aside.

Place the sole fillets in a single layer in two large frying pans. Add enough water to each pan to just cover the fillets. Begin heating over high heat. When the water comes to a boil, cover and turn down to low heat. Cook the fish about 4 minutes, or until it is firm. Try not to over-cook it.

While the fish is cooking, make the Garlicky Spinach and then set aside.

When the fish is cooked, carefully transfer each fillet to the baking sheet, using a slotted spoon, which will drain away the water. Sole is very delicate and will break into pieces easily. Spoon the cheese sauce over the fillets and sprinkle on the bread crumbs.

Heat the fish under the broiler for 2—3 minutes, or until the cheese sauce begins to brown. Remove from oven.

Spoon out 1/4 of the Garlicky Spinach onto each dinner plate and place 1 or 2 sole fillets on top. Serve immediately.

Almost Crab Cakes

Serves: 4 ✳

Preparation time: 10 minutes ✳

Cooking time: 8 minutes ✳

Time-saving tip: Use two frying pans to cook all the "crab" cakes at once. ✳

This recipe calls for Surimi, a much cheaper, though still tasty, crab-meat substitute. Don't worry that it was created in a lab. It's still seafood. These crab cakes may stay up at night wishing upon a star that one day they'll become real crab cakes. But in the meantime, they certainly taste good how they are.

1 pound imitation crab (Surimi, see page 13) (see Mom Tip)

2 large or 4 medium potatoes

4 scallions

2 large eggs

1/2 teaspoon dried dill

1/2 teaspoon salt

1/4 teaspoon black pepper

1/4 teaspoon celery seed

8 drops hot pepper sauce plus more if desired

1 tablespoon olive or corn oil plus more as needed

Cut the imitation crab into 1/4-inch pieces. Peel and grate the potatoes, using the largest grater holes. Rinse and trim the scallions and cut them into 1/4-inch pieces.

Put the imitation crab, potatoes and scallions into a large bowl. Add the eggs, dill, salt, black pepper, celery seed and hot pepper sauce and mix gently.

Put the oil into a large frying pan and begin heating over medium-high heat. Drop tablespoonfuls of the crab mixture into the pan and cook about 2 minutes per side, or until the crab cakes begin to brown.

Serve immediately or transfer to a plate and keep warm in the oven while cooking the rest of the crab cakes. Add more oil as needed.

Mom Tip: You can also use real crab if price is no object.

Coconut Shrimp Curry

Serves: 4 ✳

Preparation time: 5 minutes ✳

Cooking time: 15 minutes ✳

Time-saving tip: Use frozen chopped onions. ✳

This recipe may sound like a science experiment to you. It's the kind of recipe that started with the premise: "What would happen if you combined X, Y and Z, and then added a dash of coriander?" Well, other than making you search the dark corners of your spice rack, the result is a rather unique, tropically tinged Indian shrimp dish. Not descriptive enough? I'm afraid you're going to have to cook it to find out more.

1 large onion

2 tablespoons olive or corn oil

1 teaspoon bottled crushed garlic

1 teaspoon ground coriander

1 teaspoon ground cumin

1 teaspoon ground turmeric

1/2 teaspoon ground cinnamon

1/2 teaspoon ground chili powder

1/2 teaspoon ground ginger

1/2 teaspoon salt

1/4 teaspoon black pepper

1 cup water

1 8-ounce can tomato sauce

1 cup dried coconut (see Mom Tip)

1 pound peeled shrimp, cooked or raw

1/4 cup sour cream

Peel the onion and cut it into 1/2-inch pieces. Put the oil into a wok or large frying pan and begin heating over medium-high heat. Add the onion and cook about 5 minutes, stirring occasionally, or until the onion begins to soften.

Add the garlic, coriander, cumin, turmeric, cinnamon, chili powder, ginger, salt and black pepper and stir until the spices have dissolved. Add the water, tomato sauce and coconut and bring to a boil. Turn down to medium heat and cook, covered, for 5 minutes. Add the shrimp. If the shrimp are uncooked, cook about 3 minutes, or until they turn pink and just begin to curl. Then add the sour cream. If the shrimp are already cooked, add them and quickly stir in the sour cream. Continue heating until hot. Serve immediately or set aside until ready to eat, and then reheat briefly.

Mom Tip: Dried sweetened coconut is available in bags near the chocolate chips. Dried unsweetened coconut may be available in the Asian food aisle of the grocery store. Either type works with this dish.

Scallop Kebabs

Serves: 4 ✳

Preparation time: 15 minutes ✳

Cooking time: 10 minutes ✳

Time-saving tip: Wrap scallops in thin slices of prosciutto instead of bacon, drizzle with olive oil and broil for 2–3 minutes per side, or just until the scallops are firm and white in the middle. ✳

Scallops deserve more respect. Shrimp get all the publicity and all the cocktails, but scallops are just as good. Here they have their own chance for glory, without a shrimp in sight.

1 pound raw sea scallops (see Mom Tip 1)

1/2 pound thinly sliced bacon

Skewers

Black pepper

Preheat the broiler. Make sure the top oven rack is in the highest position, just under the broiling unit. For easy clean-up, line the broiling pan with aluminum foil. Place the broiling pan rack on top of the foil and then set aside.

Rinse the scallops under cold running water and remove and discard any small "hinges" that may be attached (see Mom Tip 2). Count the scallops. Depending on their size, there should be 30 to 40. Divide the number of scallops by three to determine how many strips of bacon you need.

Cut each bacon strip into three equal lengths. Wrap each scallop with a piece of bacon and thread it onto a metal or bamboo skewer, making sure the skewer goes through both ends of the bacon as well as the middle of the scallop. Don't cram too many scallops on each skewer. Leave at least 1/2 inch between each scallop so that the bacon will fully cook.

Lay the filled skewers on the broiling pan rack so that the bacon covering each scallop is facing up. Broil for 5 minutes. Turn the skewers over and broil another 5 minutes, or until the bacon is crisp. Season with black pepper and serve immediately.

> *Mom Tip 1: Sea scallops, which are at least 1 inch in diameter, are two or three times bigger than bay scallops. They are also much more expensive than bay scallops.*
>
> *Mom Tip 2: Scallops have a small, white, tough "hinge" on one edge, which may have already been removed at purchase. If not, remove and discard it before cooking.*

Stir-Fried Scampi

{
Serves: 4 *

Preparation time: 10 minutes *

Cooking time: 5 minutes *

Time-saving tip: Use a mini food processor to chop the parsley. *

Whenever I stir-fry, I set off the smoke alarm—it never fails. So, while trying to keep the food from burning, I have to stand on a chair and swat the alarm with a broom. Maybe it's just jealous. Stir-Fried Scampi sure does smell good when it's cooking.

6 scallions

1/2 cup fresh parsley

2 teaspoons fresh or dried rosemary

3 tablespoons butter or olive oil

2 teaspoons ground thyme

1/2 teaspoon red pepper flakes

1/4 teaspoon salt

1 tablespoon bottled crushed garlic

1 1/2 pounds cleaned raw shrimp (see Mom Tip 1)

1/4 cup bottled lemon juice

Rinse and trim the scallions and cut them into 1-inch pieces. Rinse the parsley. Cut off and discard the stems and cut the leafy parts into 1/2-inch pieces. Set the scallions and parsley aside. Crush the rosemary using a mortar and pestle or break or cut into as small pieces as possible.

Put the butter or oil into a wok or large frying pan and begin heating over high heat. Add the rosemary, thyme, red pepper flakes and salt and cook for 15 seconds. Add the garlic and stir for a few seconds. Add the shrimp and stir-fry for 2 minutes. Add the scallions and continue stir-frying another 2 minutes, or until the shrimp have turned white and are cooked through. Larger raw shrimp will take about 1 minute longer to cook. Add the lemon juice and parsley and mix well. Serve immediately.

Mom Tip 1: Raw shrimp is better for this dish than cooked shrimp because it picks up the spicy flavors during the cooking process. You can use precooked shrimp. However, if you do, add it after you have stir-fried the scallions for 30 seconds. Cook the shrimp just until they are hot and then add the lemon juice and parsley. Over-cooked shrimp will be tough.

Mom Tip 2: Stir-Fried Scampi can also be used as a sauce for pasta. Add 1 to 2 table-spoons extra butter or olive oil if it seems too dry as a sauce.

Quick Sides

When I'm in a hurry in the kitchen, the first thing that gets skipped is the side dish. I figure that an entrée-only meal is better than a side dish-only meal. But why not have it all? To address this problem, we've come up with 15 side dishes that can be made very quickly, often while the main course is cooking. Now even people in a hurry can have a well-balanced meal.

Vegetables:

Butter-Fried Cherry Tomatoes

Garlicky Spinach

Honey-Roasted Baby Carrots

Quick-Fried Cauliflower

Roasted Asparagus

10-Minute Coleslaw

Potatoes, Rice, Beans, Noodles or Bread:

Oven-Fried Baby Potatoes

Mashed Sweet Potatoes

Parmesan Potato Pancakes

Almost Instant Mexican Rice

Better-Than-Canned
Baked Beans

Toasted Barley

Orzo with Peas and Scallions

Cheesy French Garlic Bread

20-Minute Biscuits

Butter-Fried Cherry Tomatoes

Serves: 4 ✳

Preparation time: 5 minutes ✳

Cooking time: 5 minutes ✳

Time-saving tip: Use prewashed cherry tomatoes. ✳

Sometimes, when I get the urge to snack, I eat cherry tomatoes. The younger me would have reached for a bag of chips, but the new and improved (and afraid of death) me can finish a whole basket of cherry tomatoes. But I understand that most normal people wouldn't eat them that way, at least not in bulk. Butter-Fried Cherry Tomatoes is a more sensible way to prepare cherry tomatoes. I like them this way, too, although it does require that I use utensils.

1 16-ounce container cherry tomatoes (about 2 1/2 cups)

1 tablespoon butter

1 tablespoon olive or corn oil

1 teaspoon sugar

1/2 teaspoon bottled crushed garlic

1/2 teaspoon salt

1/4 teaspoon black pepper

2 tablespoons fresh parsley

Rinse the tomatoes, remove and discard any stems and pat them dry.

Put the butter and oil into a large frying pan and begin heating over medium-high heat. When the butter has melted, add the tomatoes and shake the pan so that they are covered with the butter mixture. Cook for 2 minutes and shake the pan again. The bottom side of the tomatoes will have started to brown and blister. Add the sugar, garlic, salt and black pepper and shake the pan again to distribute the seasonings. Cook another 3 minutes. The tomatoes will be soft but will still hold their shape.

While the tomatoes are cooking, rinse the parsley. Cut off and discard the stems and cut the leafy parts into 1/2-inch pieces. Sprinkle the parsley on the cooked tomatoes, shake the pan again and transfer the tomatoes to a serving dish. Serve immediately.

Garlicky Spinach

Serves: 4 *
Preparation time: 1 minute *
Cooking time: 3 minutes *
Time-saving tip: Use fresh prewashed spinach. *

How fast is fast food? Well, I guess it depends on many factors. How crowded is the restaurant? How complicated is your order? How long will the guy in front of you stare at the menu before deciding? Anyway, you'd be hard-pressed to get your food in 4 minutes. That's all this recipe takes. And, while Garlicky Spinach does taste good, it doesn't make you feel guilty.

2 tablespoons olive or corn oil

1 1/2 teaspoons bottled crushed garlic

2 6-ounce bags fresh prewashed spinach (about 16 cups)

Salt

Black pepper

Put the oil into a wok or large frying pan and begin heating over medium-high heat. Add the garlic and cook about 15 seconds. Add the spinach and cook about 2 minutes, stirring continually, or until it has wilted. Season with salt and black pepper and serve immediately.

Honey-Roasted Baby Carrots

Serves: 4 *

Preparation time: 5 minutes *

Cooking time: 20 minutes *

Time-saving tip: The thinner the carrots, the faster they cook. *

With apologies to Bugs Bunny, plain carrots can get pretty boring after a while. Here's a more adventurous alternative.

1 1-pound bag fresh baby carrots

1 tablespoon olive or corn oil

2 tablespoons honey

2 tablespoons orange juice

1/2 teaspoon bottled ginger or 1/4 teaspoon ground ginger

1/4 teaspoon salt

Place an oven rack in the middle position and preheat the oven to 475 degrees F.

Put the carrots into a large ovenproof dish and drizzle with oil. Shake the dish so that the carrots are covered with oil. Bake for 10 minutes.

While the carrots are baking, put the honey, orange juice, ginger and salt into a small bowl and mix well.

Remove the carrots from the oven, pour the honey mixture over them and shake the dish to distribute the mixture. Bake another 10 minutes, or until the carrots have begun to brown and can be pierced easily with a fork. Serve immediately or set aside until ready to eat, and then reheat briefly. These carrots are also good cold.

Quick-Fried Cauliflower

Serves: 4 ✳

Preparation time: 10 minutes ✳

Cooking time: 9 minutes ✳

Time-saving tip: Use a 16-ounce package frozen cauliflower or precut cauliflower from the grocery store's salad bar. ✳

When I prepare cauliflower, I have a tendency to spend way too much time chopping. My desire for order leads me to try to make each piece the same size. But that's virtually impossible, says my therapist. Oh well. Once the cauliflower is cut up, it's a snap to cook this way. It's one of the easiest side dishes you can make, particularly if you don't have my issues.

1 small or 1/2 large cauliflower

3 tablespoons olive or corn oil

1 teaspoon ground coriander

1 teaspoon ground cumin

1/2 teaspoon salt

1/2 teaspoon ground turmeric

1/2 teaspoon black pepper

1/4 teaspoon cayenne pepper

Trim and discard the leaves and core from the cauliflower. Cut the rest into bite-size pieces.

Put the oil into a large frying pan or wok and begin heating over medium-high heat. Add the cauliflower and cook about 3 minutes, stirring occasionally, until some of the pieces begin to brown. Turn down to low heat, cover and cook about 5 minutes, shaking the pan occasionally, or until the cauliflower has begun to soften but not gone limp.

While the cauliflower is cooking, put the coriander, cumin, salt, turmeric, black pepper and cayenne pepper into a small cup and mix well. When the cauliflower is done cooking, sprinkle it with the spice mixture and stir-fry for 1 minute. Serve immediately or set aside until ready to eat, and then reheat briefly.

Roasted Asparagus

Serves: 4

Preparation time: 5 minutes

Cooking time: 10–15 minutes

Time-saving tip: Thin asparagus cooks more quickly than fat asparagus.

This is the perfect way to prepare a side dish if you're already baking something. Asparagus, or as my grandmother pronounces it, "asparagarus," completes any meal. Even if you've made yourself a huge mound of french fries for dinner, as long as you eat your asparagus you'll feel good about yourself.

1 pound asparagus

2 tablespoons olive or corn oil

1/2 teaspoon salt

1/4 teaspoon black pepper

Place an oven rack in the middle position and preheat the oven to 425 degrees F. Line a roasting pan with aluminum foil for easy cleanup.

Rinse the asparagus under cold running water. Snap off and discard the bottom inch or two of the stalks. Put the asparagus into the roasting pan and drizzle the oil over top. Sprinkle with salt and black pepper.

Put the roasting pan into the oven and every 5 minutes, shake the pan. This motion will help the asparagus cook more evenly. After 10 minutes, try to pierce 1 stalk with the tip of a sharp knife. If you can easily pierce the stalk, the asparagus is ready. If not, let it bake 1–2 minutes more and test again.

When the asparagus is done, transfer it to a serving dish and serve immediately or set aside until ready to eat, and then reheat briefly. It is also good cold.

10-Minute Coleslaw

Serves: 4 ✳

Preparation time: 10 minutes ✳

Cooking time: none ✳

Time-saving tip: Use a bottled vinaigrette salad dressing instead of making your own. ✳

Coleslaw is the great American side dish. It's a staple food of cookouts, pot lucks and retirement parties. It usually takes at least 30 minutes to make, but not anymore. By buying precut cabbage you not only save time chopping, but you don't have to search all the drawers in the kitchen for the "shredding" blade for your food processor. I think my wife hides ours.

1 16-ounce bag shredded cabbage

1/4 cup mayonnaise

2 tablespoons red wine vinegar

1 teaspoon sugar

1 teaspoon Dijon mustard

1/2 teaspoon salt

1/4 teaspoon dried celery seeds

1/4 teaspoon black pepper

1/8 teaspoon hot pepper sauce

Put the shredded cabbage into a large bowl. Add the mayonnaise, vinegar, sugar, mustard, salt, celery seeds, black pepper and hot pepper sauce and mix well. Serve immediately or cover and refrigerate until ready to eat.

Oven-Fried Baby Potatoes

Serves: 4 ✳

Preparation time: 5 minutes ✳

Cooking time: 15 minutes ✳

Time-saving tip: Peel and cut larger potatoes into 1/4-inch slices. They will be ready a few minutes sooner. ✳

These potatoes will happily fry themselves in the oven while you do other things. There's no need to stand over them, watching them, flipping them, whispering encouraging words to them. Just close the oven door and do 15 minutes of jumping jacks. The jumping jacks are optional.

12 small (2-inch diameter) Gold Yukon, White Rose or Red Rose potatoes (see Mom Tip)

2 tablespoons olive or corn oil

1/2 teaspoon dried oregano

1/4 teaspoon salt

1/4 teaspoon black pepper

Place an oven rack in the middle position and preheat the oven to 400 degrees F. For easy clean-up, line a baking sheet with aluminum foil.

Scrub the potatoes, cut them in half and put them into a bowl. Drizzle them with oil and then sprinkle oregano, salt and black pepper over top and toss gently. Place the potatoes cut-side down on the baking sheet and bake for 15 minutes, or until they can be pierced easily with a knife. Serve immediately or keep warm until needed.

Mom Tip: Yukon Gold, White Rose and Red Rose potatoes hold their shape better when cooked this way, but any potato can be used. Cut large potatoes into 1-inch slices. If you use russet or Idaho potatoes, peel them first.

Mashed Sweet Potatoes

Serves: 4 ✳

Preparation time: 6 minutes ✳

Cooking time: 10 minutes ✳

Time-saving tip: The thinner you cut the sweet potato slices, the faster they cook. ✳

I remember being told as a child that sweet potatoes were the candy version of regular potatoes. I don't know which adult it was who told me that lie, but there were only two of them in the house, so an investigation wouldn't need to be too extensive. The truth is, my parents needn't have lied to me. I would have liked them anyway. Mashed Sweet Potatoes are really good. They're the candy version of regular mashed potatoes.

1 1/2 pounds sweet potatoes or yams (see Mom Tip 1)

3 to 4 tablespoons maple syrup

2 tablespoons butter

1/2 teaspoon salt

1/4 teaspoon black pepper

Peel the sweet potatoes and cut them into 1/4-inch slices. Put the slices into a medium pot and add water up to the depth of 1 inch. The water does not have to cover the potatoes. Cover and cook over medium-high heat about 10 minutes, or until the potato slices are very soft.

Drain and mash with a fork. Add the maple syrup, butter, salt and black pepper and mix well. Serve immediately. Or set aside until ready to eat, and then reheat briefly.

Mom Tip 1: Sweet potatoes and yams can be used interchangeably for this dish, and the taste will be similar. But somehow, "Mashed Yams" doesn't sound quite as delicious. Sweet potatoes and yams have a similar long shape, often with pointed ends. The skin of sweet potatoes is light brown, and the flesh is pale yellow. The skin of yams is orange or reddish-brown, and the flesh is orange. Yams are slightly sweeter than sweet potatoes, but both are much sweeter than regular potatoes.

Mom Tip 2: To add extra flavor, cook 1 cup chopped pecans in 2 tablespoons butter over medium heat about 5 minutes, or until the pecans begin to brown, and pour over the top of the Mashed Sweet Potatoes.

Parmesan Potato Pancakes

Serves: 4 ✳

Preparation time: 10–12 minutes ✳

Cooking time: 12 minutes ✳

Time-saving tip: Use Yukon Gold, Red Rose or White Rose potatoes; you just have to scrub them, not peel them. ✳

Parmesan Potato Pancakes resemble breakfast pancakes only in that they're flat and round. What they are is an exciting opportunity to use some of the fancy attachments on your food processor. I'm not generally into power tools, but there is something satisfying about watching the potatoes, onions and artichoke hearts bend to your will in the Cuisinart. All that remains is a little mixing and you're ready to cook. It's that simple.

2 medium potatoes (about 3/4 pound)

1 small onion

3 canned artichoke hearts

1 large egg

3 tablespoons grated Parmesan cheese

2 tablespoons flour plus more if needed

1/2 teaspoon baking powder

1/2 teaspoon salt

2 tablespoons olive or corn oil plus more if needed

Sour cream (optional)

Peel the potatoes and onion. Grate the potatoes, onion and artichoke hearts in a food processor, using the shredding blade. Or shred the potatoes and onion using a hand grater, and cut the artichoke hearts into slivers with a knife.

Put the potatoes, onion and artichoke hearts into a medium bowl. Add the egg, Parmesan cheese, flour, baking powder and salt and mix well. If the mixture seems runny, add up to 1 more tablespoon flour.

Put the oil into a large frying pan and begin heating over medium-high heat. Add tablespoonfuls of potato mixture to the pan and flatten them with the back of the spoon so they are about 2 inches across. Cook about 3 minutes per side, or until both sides are brown.

Remove the pancakes from the pan and drain on a paper towel. Continue cooking more pancakes, adding more oil as needed, until they are all cooked. Serve immediately with sour cream, if using, or keep warm on a plate in the oven until needed.

Almost Instant Mexican Rice

Serves: 4 *

Preparation time: 5 minutes *

Cooking time: 20 minutes *

Time-saving tip: Boil the water in the microwave. *

It's great to be able to enliven a bowl of rice simply by adding a condiment. I wish all cooking were this easy. I would be an instant gourmet if only I could find recipes that used the relish, mustard, ketchup, etc., that litter my fridge. Unfortunately, most recipes actually require that I go to the grocery store. But this recipe was a great find.

1 1/2 cups water

1 cup fresh or bottled salsa, divided

1 cup long-grain white rice

1/2 teaspoon salt

Put the water into a medium pot, cover and bring to a boil over high heat. Add half the salsa, rice and salt and return the water to a boil. Stir, cover and turn down to low heat. Cook 15 minutes. Remove from heat, add the remaining salsa and let the rice sit, covered, another 5 minutes to finish cooking. Stir and serve immediately or set aside until ready to eat, and then reheat briefly.

Better-Than-Canned Baked Beans

Serves: 4 ✳

Preparation time: 10 minutes ✳

Cooking time: 5 minutes ✳

Time-saving tip: Use 1 cup barbecue sauce instead of ketchup, molasses, brown sugar, mustard and Worcestershire sauce. ✳

I associate baked beans with a thousand old Westerns. It seems like it was the only thing they ate back then. Did those rugged gunslingers and bear wrestlers carry Worcestershire sauce with them on cattle drives? Maybe this is a more civilized version.

2 15-ounce cans cannellini, pinto
   or Great Northern beans

1/2 cup ketchup

1/4 cup dried minced onion

1/4 cup dark molasses (see Mom Tip)

1 tablespoon brown sugar

1 tablespoon Dijon mustard

1 tablespoon Worcestershire sauce

1/2 teaspoon salt

1/4 teaspoon black pepper

Drain the beans, rinse them under cold running water and put them into a medium pot. Add the ketchup, onion, molasses, brown sugar, mustard, Worcestershire sauce, salt and black pepper and mix well. Bring the mixture to a boil, turn down to medium heat and cook, uncovered, for 5 minutes. If the bean mixture seems too dry, add 1 to 2 tablespoons water. Serve immediately or set aside until ready to eat, and then reheat briefly.

Mom Tip: Molasses is available near the pancake syrup at the grocery store.

Toasted Barley

Serves: 4 ✳

Preparation time: 5 minutes ✳

Cooking time: 18—20 minutes

Time-saving tip: Heat water in microwave. ✳

I thought my mom had gone off the hippie deep-end when she offered me some toasted barley. It sounded so wholesome and natural that I assumed it would taste bad. But it actually tastes good, and is an easy alternative to rice.

3 cups water

2 tablespoons olive or corn oil

1 cup pearl barley (see Mom Tip 1)

1/2 teaspoon salt

Put the water into a medium pot, cover and bring to a boil over high heat.

Put the oil into a medium pot and begin heating over medium-high heat. Add the barley and cook, stirring frequently, about 3 minutes, or until some of it starts to brown. Add the boiling water and salt and continue cooking, uncovered, for 10 minutes, stirring occasionally. Turn down to medium heat and cook another 5 minutes. The barley will begin to swell as it absorbs the water. Taste a kernel to see if it's tender; it will be slightly chewy. If yes, remove from heat, cover and then set aside until needed; if not, continue cooking for 2–3 more minutes and test again. It should be ready by the time all the water is absorbed. If not, add 1 to 2 more tablespoons water. If any water remains, drain and discard before serving.

> **Mom Tip 1:** *Pearl barley is often available in 1-pound bags in the rice aisle, near the dried lentils and other dried beans. Or it may be in the organic food section. It's a good alternative to rice.*

> **Mom Tip 2:** *To make this dish more elaborate, cook 1/2 to 1 pound presliced mushrooms in 2 tablespoons butter or oil about 5 minutes, or until they soften. Drain the mushrooms, discarding the liquid, and add them to the cooked barley just before serving.*

Orzo with Peas and Scallions

Serves: 4 ✳

Preparation time: 5 minutes ✳

Cooking time: 2 minutes plus 9 minutes for the orzo

Time-saving tip: Use frozen chopped onions instead of scallions and add them when you add the peas. ✳

What is orzo? It's a pasta that looks like rice and cooks twice as fast, and it mixes well with vegetables or in soups. As a kid, the only reason I asked for chicken soup was because my mom would put orzo (I didn't know what it was called) in it. I would suck down the soup and then slowly enjoy the pile of little noodles at the bottom. But orzo can also be the main attraction. If you like, you could eat the peas and scallions first, leaving the orzo till last. But I don't think that's necessary.

3 scallions

1 cup uncooked orzo

1 cup frozen peas

1 tablespoon olive or corn oil

1/2 teaspoon salt

1/4 teaspoon black pepper

Handful fresh prewashed spinach or arugula (optional)

Fill a medium pot with water, cover and begin heating over high heat.

Rinse and trim the scallions and cut them into 1/2-inch pieces and then set aside.

When the water comes to a boil, add the orzo and cook according to directions. About 4 minutes before the orzo is done, add the peas to the water.

Meanwhile, put the oil into a large frying pan or wok and begin heating over medium-high heat. Add the scallions and cook about 1 minute, stirring occasionally, or until they begin to soften. Remove from heat.

When the orzo and peas are cooked, drain them and add them to the scallions. Add the salt and black pepper and, if using, the spinach or arugula. Stir until the greens wilt. Serve immediately or set aside until ready to eat, and then reheat briefly.

Cheesy French Garlic Bread

Serves: 4 ✳

Preparation time: 6 minutes ✳

Cooking time: 18 minutes ✳

Time-saving tip: Use grated cheese. ✳

I like to take my toddler Sammy for walks to a terrific bakery in my neighborhood. We buy a two-foot loaf of French bread and stuff our faces all the way home. I don't know which of us eats more, but we're generally down to about one foot by the time we get back. With the remaining half I tend to make garlic bread. This variation is a family favorite.

2 tablespoons butter

2 tablespoons olive oil

1 tablespoon salad seasoning (see Mom Tip)

2 teaspoons bottled crushed garlic

1/4 pound sliced mozzarella, muenster or Monterey Jack cheese

1 baguette-style French bread

Place an oven rack in the middle position and preheat the oven to 425 degrees F.

Melt the butter and oil in a small pot over medium-high heat. Remove from heat and add the salad seasoning and garlic and then set aside.

Cut the French bread in half horizontally so you have two long, thin strips. Spoon the butter mixture onto the two cut sides of the bread. Lay slices of cheese on one side and put the other strip of bread, cut side down, on top, sandwich style. Wrap the bread tightly in aluminum foil, making sure it is completely enclosed, and bake for 15 minutes. Then open the foil and bake another 3 minutes to crisp up the bread. Remove from oven and cut into 2-inch slices, keeping the top and bottom slices together. Serve immediately.

Mom Tip: *To make your own salad seasoning, use 1 1/2 teaspoons Parmesan cheese, 1 teaspoon dried oregano, 1/4 teaspoon paprika and 1/4 teaspoon dried celery seeds.*

20-Minute Biscuits

Serves: 4 ✳

Preparation time: 5 minutes ✳

Cooking time: 15 minutes ✳

Time-saving tip: Bake at a higher temperature (see Mom Tip). ✳

I guess if we call something 20-Minute Biscuits, we better be right on the mark. I've made these biscuits at least five times, and only once did it take longer than 20 minutes. That was the time that I realized halfway through that I didn't have any milk and had to rush to the minimart. So, a few scared pedestrians and several tense seconds while I fumbled for change in my pocket later, the biscuits were done in 27 minutes. Otherwise, the name is accurate.

1 cup flour

1/2 cup milk

2 tablespoons mayonnaise

1 teaspoon baking powder

1/2 teaspoon salt

Place an oven rack in the middle position and preheat the oven to 425 degrees F (see Mom Tip). Line a baking sheet with aluminum foil for easy cleanup.

Put the flour, milk, mayonnaise, baking powder and salt into a medium bowl and mix well. The mixture will be sticky.

Scoop out 1 heaping teaspoon of dough and drop it onto the foil on the baking sheet. Repeat until all the dough is used up. There should be 10 to 12 biscuits.

Bake for 15 minutes, or until the tops of the biscuits have begun to brown. Remove from oven. When cool enough to handle, pull the biscuits from the foil and serve.

Mom Tip: The baking time and temperature can be adjusted to coordinate with other parts of the dinner you may be baking. For instance, you can bake these biscuits at 375 degrees F for 20 minutes or 400 degrees F for about 18 minutes.

Vegetable, Potato & Rice Basics

Vegetables:

Boiling

Roasting

Stir-Frying

Potatoes:

Boiled or Mashed

French Fries

Shredded and Fried

Rice and Couscous:

Plain Rice

Brown Rice

Couscous

Vegetables

Many fresh vegetables can be cooked in minutes using simple boiling, roasting and stir-frying techniques. You probably already know everything I'm going to tell you, but maybe a quick skim-through will give you some ideas about quick side dishes not spelled out in this book. Cooking times are given in parentheses. I prefer my vegetables crisp rather than mushy.

For a simple sauce, add 1 to 2 tablespoons butter to any hot cooked (and well-drained) vegetable and season with salt and black pepper.

For a stronger flavored sauce, season with garlic salt, onion salt or salad seasoning.

For a spicier effect, melt 1 tablespoon butter and 1 tablespoon olive or corn oil in a large frying pan or wok. Add 1 teaspoon bottled crushed garlic and 1/4 teaspoon red pepper flakes and then cook for 30 seconds. Add the vegetables and stir. You can also use fresh or bottled salsa as a quick topping for almost any cooked vegetable.

Cook any of the following in 1-inch boiling water (except for corn-on-the-cob and green beans, which should be submerged in boiling water). Vegetables are done when you can pierce them (not too easily) with a knife.

Boiling

Asparagus (3–5 minutes, depending on thickness)

Broccoli (about 5 minutes)

Brussels sprouts (about 7 minutes for small sprouts)

Carrots (sliced, about 5 minutes; whole, about 15 minutes)

Caullflower (about 7 minutes)

Corn-on-the-cob (about 2 minutes)

Green beans (about 5 minutes)

Snow peas (about 1 minute)

Zucchini (about 2 minutes)

Roasting

Heat the oven to 450 degrees F. Cut bell peppers, carrots, eggplant, onions and zucchini into 1 1/2-inch pieces. Asparagus and mushrooms can remain whole. Put vegetable(s) into a roasting pan and drizzle with olive oil. Season with salt and black pepper and roast about 20 minutes. Vegetables are done when you can pierce them (not too easily) with a knife.

Stir-Frying

Cut any of the following into bite-size pieces or strips and cook in 1 to 2 tablespoons olive or corn oil over high heat, stirring constantly. Most vegetables will be done in about 2 minutes, although carrots and onions will take a few minutes longer.

Asparagus

Bell peppers

Broccoli

Cabbage

Carrots

Cauliflower

Cherry tomatoes (can remain whole)

Green beans (can remain whole)

Mushrooms (can remain whole)

Onions

Snow peas (can remain whole)

Spinach

Zucchini

There are many ways to cook potatoes so they will be ready to eat in 25 minutes or less. Take your pick.

Boiled or Mashed Potatoes (serves 4)

Peel 4 large potatoes and cut them into 1 1/2-inch pieces. Put them into a medium or large pot, cover with water and bring to a boil over high heat. Turn down to medium heat and cook, covered, about 20 minutes, or until easily pierced with a fork. Drain.

For boiled potatoes, add 2 tablespoons butter and, if you like, 2 tablespoons chopped parsley. When the butter has melted, toss. Season with salt and black pepper and serve.

For mashed potatoes, add 1/2 cup hot milk and 2 tablespoons butter. When the butter has melted, mash with a fork or potato masher. Season with salt and black pepper and serve. To vary the flavor, add 2 tablespoons Parmesan cheese or 1 tablespoon horseradish during the mashing process.

French Fries (serves 4)

Peel 3 large potatoes and cut them into 1/2-inch slices. Cut the slices into 1/2-inch-wide strips. Heat 3 tablespoons corn or olive oil in a large frying pan over high heat. Add the potatoes and cook for 10–15 minutes, turning frequently, until they are brown. Drain on paper towels and serve immediately.

Shredded and Fried Potatoes (serves 4)

Peel 3 large potatoes and grate them, using the shredding blade of your food processor or largest holes of your grater. Heat 3 tablespoons corn oil in a large frying pan over medium-high heat. Add the potatoes and cook about 10 minutes, turning occasionally, until they are brown. Serve immediately.

—————————— Rice and Couscous ——————————

Plain rice is probably the easiest side dish to make because it practically cooks itself. Just add water, heat and a lid. Mistakes occur if there is too little water (the rice doesn't get soft enough) or too much heat (the rice burns on the bottom) or too little heat (the rice is not ready when you want to serve it). Too much water is not a problem. Just pour off any excess when the rice is done.

As for instant rice, yes, it's ready in a few minutes. But then you have to actually eat it. Unless it's covered with a very flavorful sauce, I'd rather eat shredded cardboard. There are many varieties of white rice, but for cooking purposes, the main consideration is the length of the rice grain. Any long-grain rice, which includes Basmati, Jasmine and Carolina, can be cooked in the same way—1 cup rice to 2 cups water. Short-grain rice, which includes Asian rices and Italian rices such as Arborio—is cooked in less water. Because it has more starch, this rice will be sticky and will clump together, making it easy to eat with chopsticks.

Follow the directions on the package, but here are basic recipes that should work for each type of rice.

Plain Rice (serves 4)

Put 2 cups water into a medium pot, cover and bring to a boil over high heat. Add 1 cup long-grain white rice, stir, cover and turn down to low heat. Cook for 15 minutes and then remove from heat and let sit 5 minutes to finish cooking.

Put 1 1/3 cups water into a medium pot, cover and bring to a boil over high heat. Add 1 cup short-grain white rice, stir, cover and turn down to low heat. Cook for 15 minutes and then remove from heat and let sit 5 minutes to finish cooking.

Brown Rice (serves 4)

Brown rice normally takes considerably longer to cook. However, here is a way to cook it so that it is ready in about 25 minutes. The rice might be slightly chewier than you're used to, but it is an agreeable alternative to white rice.

Bring 2 cups water to a boil over high heat. Meanwhile, heat 2 tablespoons butter or olive oil in a medium pot over medium-high heat. When the butter has melted or the oil is hot, add 1 cup brown rice and cook, stirring frequently, for 5 minutes, or until the rice begins to brown. Add the boiling water, cover and turn down to medium heat. Cook about 20 minutes, or until the water has been absorbed and the rice is soft enough to eat. Check after 15 minutes to make sure all the water hasn't all been absorbed. If it has, taste the rice. If it's too chewy, add 1/4 cup more boiling water and continue cooking another 5 minutes or more, until it is the consistency you like. Add a few more tablespoons water if necessary. Serve immediately.

Couscous (serves 4)

Couscous is the quickest grain to cook. White and whole wheat varieties are available in boxes either near the rice or in the ethnic foods aisle.

Combine 1 cup boiling water, 1 tablespoon butter and 1 cup couscous in a bowl or pot, cover and let sit 5 minutes. Stir and serve immediately or reheat in the microwave when ready to serve.

Our Favorite Emergency Meals

I've been eating dinner for 34 years, so you'd think I'd have a pretty good idea it was coming up every night. Yet sometimes dinnertime catches me by complete surprise. At moments like these, it's nice to have some emergency meals. Here are some of our favorite recipes that you can make with ingredients we advise you keep in your pantry, refrigerator and freezer.

Soups

Salads

Sandwiches & Tortillas

Eggs & Cheese

Pasta

Rice, Beans, Grains & Tofu

Poultry

Meat

Fish & Shellfish

Quick Sides

Time Charts

The whole purpose of this book is cooking with speed. But even in this book there's fast and there's light speed. In this section we've broken down the recipes into categories, ranging from really fast food to foods that take a little more time.

15 Minutes or Less

Salads

Sandwiches & Tortillas

Eggs & Cheese

Poultry

Meat

Fish & Shellfish

Quick Sides

20 Minutes

Soups

Salads

Sandwiches & Tortillas

Eggs & Cheese

Pasta

Rice, Beans, Grains & Tofu

Poultry

Meat

Fish & Shellfish

Quick Sides

25 Minutes

Soups

Salads

Sandwiches & Tortillas

Eggs & Cheese

Pasta

Rice, Beans, Grains & Tofu

Poultry

Meat

Stocking Your Pantry

Unless you're one of those people with a basement full of tuna fish in preparation for the apocalypse, your pantry may need a little bulking up. If you keep certain foods around, you'll always be able to make yourself a meal on a moment's notice. Here are some ideas for foods to keep on hand.

Pantry

Artichoke hearts (canned)

Baking powder

Beans (canned black, kidney, garbanzo, cannellini or other white beans)

Beer

Black bean garlic sauce

Bouillon cubes

Broth (canned chicken, beef and vegetable)

Capers (canned)

Clams (canned)

Corn (canned)

Cornstarch

Couscous

Dried bread crumbs

Dried coconut

Dried shiitake mushrooms

Evaporated milk (canned)

Flour (all-purpose)

Green chiles, diced (canned)

Honey

Kalamata olives (canned)

Ketchup

Kipper fillets (canned)

Lemon juice

Lentils

Mayonnaise

Mustard (regular and Dijon)

Oil (olive, corn, peanut and sesame)

Onions (red and yellow)

Pasta (spaghetti, linguine, vermicelli. penne, fusilli, orzo, tortellini)

Pearl barley

Peanut butter

Potatoes

Raisins

Rice (long-grain, Arborio)

Roasted red peppers

Salsa

Salmon (canned)

Skewers

Soy sauce

Spaghetti sauce

Sugar (granulated and brown)

Tomatoes (15-ounce ready-cut)

Tomato sauce (8-ounce)

Tuna fish (packed in water and imported tuna in olive oil)

Vinegar (balsamic, cider, red wine and white)

Wine (dry white, red)

Worcestershire sauce

Seasonings

Black pepper

Cayenne pepper

Dried basil

Dried dill

Dried oregano

Dried thyme

Garam masala

Garlic powder

Ground chili powder

Ground coriander

Ground cumin

Ground ginger

Ground turmeric

Hot pepper sauce

Minced onion

Paprika

Red pepper flakes

Salt

Refrigerator

Butter
Eggs (large)
Feta cheese
Milk

Celery
Scallions
Peeled baby carrots
Sour cream
Surimi (vacuum-sealed package)

Bottled crushed garlic
Bottled ginger

Freezer

Bacon (wrapped in 4-slice packages)
Boneless chicken breasts (individually wrapped)
Bread
Fish fillets
Ground turkey or ground chicken (1-pound packages)
Scallops

Shrimp
Sirloin steak

Grated cheddar or Monterey Jack cheese
Grated mozzarella cheese
Grated Parmesan cheese

Bell peppers (precut)
Cauliflower
Corn
Onions (precut)
Peas
Spinach

Hamburger buns
Pine nuts
Tortillas

Index

About the Authors

Kevin Mills is a 1993 graduate of Cornell University, with a major in history. He is the co-author of *HELP! My Apartment Has a Kitchen*, *HELP! My Apartment Has a Dining Room* and *Chocolate on the Brain*. He is a regular contributor to *Parents Magazine*, writing humorous pieces on child-raising.

Nancy Mills is a 1964 graduate of Cornell University, with a major in home economics. She is the co-author of *HELP! My Apartment Has a Kitchen*, *HELP! My Apartment Has a Dining Room* and *Chocolate on the Brain*. She is the co-author (with Bart Mills) of *Beverly Hills 90210: Exposed* and *Melrose Place: Off the Record*. She is a regular contributor to the entertainment sections of the *New York Daily News*, *USA Weekend Magazine* and *YOU Magazine* in England.